Skiing

Rosi Mittermaier and Christian Neureuther

Springfield Books Limited

We would like to thank the following companies: ADIDAS, INDAGO, JETSTAR, KITEX, REUSCH and VÖLKL, and also the parish of Sölden, without whose generous support we could never have produced such a colourful book.

Acknowledgements

Design and layout: Yves Buchheim
Illustrations: Heinz Bogner
Cover design:
Douglas Martin Associates
Cover photos: Christian Perret
English translation:
Andrew Shackleton/
Alder Translation Services
Skiing adviser on English edition:
John Shedden,
Director of Coaching,
English Ski Council

Mittermaier, Rosi
  Skiing.
  1. Skis and skiing
  I. Title II. Neureuther, Christian
  III. Messmann, Kuno   IV. Unser
  Skibuch, *English*
  796.93   GV854

  ISBN 0–947655–00–X

Film setting: Paul Hicks Limited, Oakfield Press, Plymouth, Devon

Reproduction: SKU Reproduktionen GmbH & Co. KG, Munich, W.G.

Printed in Germany by Mohndruck Graphische Betriebe GmbH

ISBN: 0 947655 00 X

Contents

Life at the top

by Harry Valérien

Rosi and Christian were every reporter's dream. No one was as straightforward as Rosi or as good value as Christian. At 25, Rosi's rise to fame came rather late. Up to then she had spoken very little in public, giving the odd brief interview following her many wins in national championships. Two people inspired Rosi more than any others. First, her older sister Heidi, whom she emulated in everything. Heidi won in both big and small events, and in 1960 reached the Winter Olympics in America, where she got to know all the big stars of Alpine skiing. Secondly, from the age of 13 Rosi wanted to be like Barbi Henneberger: beautiful, intelligent, talented and successful. Once, when her leg was in plaster, she asked Barbi to autograph it. "That really made my day . . ." But at first her father had discouraged her from competitive skiing. It was only when Heidi withdrew after the 1966 World Championships that she was allowed to start. While other competitors trained avidly, Rosi was more relaxed about it. From the very beginning she took things easily and naturally. Not that she didn't want to win — far from it! At the 1968 Winter Olympics in Grenoble, for example, she spray-painted her skis in red so that no one would know she had changed to a different make of ski just before the race. At that time, however, she was well down in the team and could hardly dream of winning medals. The winners that year were Marielle Goitschel, Nancy Greene and Olga Pall. If you mentioned the name Mittermaier, people thought you were talking about Heidi, although she was no longer in the running. But four years later in Sapporo, Rosi surprised everyone by coming sixth in the downhill. Her World Cup wins, though, were always in other events.

Christian's manner was quite different from Rosi's. He was never shy or lost for words, and obviously enjoyed a good chat. Indeed, he never stopped talking, and had an answer for everything, even when journalists asked him why he had lost a race. He always looked as if he was waiting for the champagne. Christian Neureuther always had something to say about himself and his rivals, and about the officials too. Whenever there was a pause he would launch in with something new. It goes without saying that he achieved a lot more on the *piste* than his critics would have liked. Twelve times German champion and at the top of the world class for nearly a decade, he was triumphant in victory and cheerful in defeat. Christian Neureuther gave up his medical training shortly before the pre-medical exams. He wanted to spend the winter skiing rather than dissecting corpses at university. He later toyed with the idea of becoming a journalist or a sports teacher, and for two terms he studied art history like his mother before him. As the son of a hospital

Fun together at the photo sessions for this book

consultant, his career would appear to have been mapped out from an early age. "But the marvellous thing about my parents was that they never pushed me into a particular career or profession. They never pressurised me. And because I hadn't achieved what I wanted to in skiing, I simply stayed on in the sport. I never found a more profitable occupation than skiing ..."

Christian started too late to be able to make the best use of his talents or to realise his full potential. It was only when Heinz Mohr took over the physical training of the team that he

Christian aged four, trying out his first pair of skis

never had the necessary nerves of steel, either mentally or emotionally. And in this he was different from all the really successful skiers, Rosi herself included. Christian is one of those restless individuals who are always on the lookout for some new project: a new career as a television personality;

doing deals with a ski manufacturer; signing a contract with a wine producer; recording for a new LP; meeting with a hotel firm to finalise arrangements for a conference; coaching ski instructors; playing football for charity; flying to Canada for a cross-country event; returning to discuss a book project with a publisher and arrange photo sessions. He says of himself, "I want to work independently. And I think I can make a go of it, thanks to my sporting career. OK, sometimes I'm still a bit wild, going from one extreme to the other — but things are already looking up. Rosi isn't interested in money. Her priorities are family, health and having enough to eat. But I want to make something of myself. I'm ambitious, and I want to achieve something. At first it was rather traumatic for me, being Rosi's 'other half' — 'Mr Mittermaier'. But I've got over that now, because I know we love and understand each other on a different

Rosi and Christian pictured following their first joint victory at the 1967 German Championships

Rosi aged three and a half, skiing for the very first time

began to work really hard. He did achieve six World Cup victories, beating Gustav Thöni, Piero Gros, Fernandez Ochoa, Phil Mahre, Ingemar Stenmark and all the other slalom winners of his time; but he was not destined for a World Championship victory or an Olympic gold. He was subject to disturbing thoughts and feelings which caused him to lack decisiveness; he also

basis. I'll say it again: I like this way of life. One day I expect I'll be glad that I once appeared as 'Torero' on Dalli-Dalli [a television show]. But for the moment, every hour of the day or night I'm thinking of all the new things we could do in our life."

Marriages and friendships often suffer from the monotony of everyday life. Rosi need not, and does not, complain. For her, skiing has always been a sideline, a hobby. She wanted to travel, and to exchange her home life for the exotic scenes and new faces of other lands. She saw this as a form of preparation for later life.

Rosi aged 17 at her Olympic debut

Rosi has always had a talent for riding over the unpleasant things in life and never letting them get her down. I have never heard her complain, either about herself or about anyone else. She once said to me, "I do everything because I want to. Nobody pushes me into anything. Maybe that's why I'm so easy and relaxed about things . . ."

Christian had a difficult time winning Rosi. He had only met her once when

Rosi Mittermaier: *highlights*

Born on 5 August 1950 in Reit im Winkl, and grew up on the Winklmoosalm

1954 — first skiing attempts
1956 — first victory in junior races at Reit im Winkl
1959 — first races at a regional level
1965 — enters the German national team
1966 — German Junior Champion in the slalom, giant slalom and combined disciplines
1967 — German Champion in the slalom and combined disciplines; promoted to the first start group at international events
1968 — Winter Olympics at Grenoble — comes 11th in the giant slalom
1969 — first victory in the World Cup slalom at Schruns
1970 — World Championships at Gröden — comes 7th in the giant slalom and 5th in combined disciplines
1972 — Winter Olympics at Sapporo — comes 6th.in the downhill
1974 — World Championships at St Moritz
1976 — Winter Olympics at Innsbruck
 — gold medal in the downhill
 — gold medal in the slalom
 — silver medal in the giant slalom
 three times World Champion "Sportswoman of the Year"
1979 — member of the demonstration team sent by the German Ski Instructors' Association to the International Skiing Congress in Japan

Altogether 9 World Cup victories and 16 times German Champion
Fully qualified ski instructor since 1979

Christian Neureuther: *highlights*

Born on 28 April 1949 in Garmisch-Partenkirchen Grammar-school and university education

1953 — first skiing attempts
1955 — trained at Partenkirchen Ski Club
 first victory in junior races
1959 — first races at a regional level
1965 — member of the German junior national team
1967 — Bavarian Junior Champion in the downhill, slalom and combined disciplines
1969 — German Champion for the first time in the slalom
1970 — World Championships at Gröden
 wins the World Student Championships in Finland
1972 — Winter Olympics at Sapporo — comes 11th in the slalom
1973 — first World Cup victory in the slalom at Wengen; second in the World Cup average in the slalom
1974 — World Championships at St. Moritz; second in the World Cup average in the slalom
1976 — Winter Olympics at Innsbruck — comes 5th in the slalom
1978 — World Championships at Garmisch-Partenkirchen — comes 6th in the slalom
1979 — third in the World Cup average in the slalom
1980 — Winter Olympics at Lake Placid — comes 5th in the slalom: third in the World Cup average in the slalom

Altogether 6 World Cup victories, most notably at Kitzbühel in 1979, and 12 times German Champion
Fully qualified ski instructor since 1979

he decided to lay it on the line to his girlfriend Gabi. "I was sitting in my parents' bedroom, and I called out to her: 'We're going to have to break it off now. I've met this girl and I'm really fond of her — so there's no sense in us going on together!' Two years later, in 1968, I knew that Rosi was going to be my wife . . ."

Sick people used to travel to Kitzbühel to see Toni Sailer, thinking that a three-times Olympic champion could heal them by laying hands on them. But the magic of Rosi Mittermaier lies in the openness of her face and in her warm, friendly laugh. At the 1972 Winter Olympics in Sapporo, the Japanese treated her like a beloved princess, paying homage to her and showering her with gifts. And once during the same period, the Canadian Betsy Clifford remarked to her, "I'd almost prefer you to win, because you laugh so beautifully . . ."

It was in Innsbruck in 1976 that she received her greatest accolade, having won two gold medals and one silver. Many observers wondered how she would cope with this change in her life. I met her on the last Sunday of the competition at the entrance to the Olympic village. The harassment from the public and the press seemed to have taken its toll on her already: she seemed listless and exhausted. We jumped into a minibus and headed for town — the only way to have a relatively undisturbed conversation. I asked Rosi how she managed to cope with all the hassle. "I just switch off and stop listening; I'm aware of what's going on around me, but I can't really

[top] Rosi skis to victory in the downhill at Innsbruck

[bottom] Rosi with her three Olympic medals

12

take it in or make anything of it. Good heavens! What would it have been like if I'd won *three* gold medals?"

I shall never forget the scene which followed her win in the Axamer Lizum. An assistant from the American TV company ABC, about six foot three tall, saw her being crushed by the throng. Without hesitation he lifted her up high and carried her like a doll through the deep, powdery snow to his American colleagues. Rosi was helpless against the whims of the public. But as I suggested afterwards, this was only for a relatively short period of her life: "She will soon be able to decide for herself where she wants to go, whom she wishes to speak to, and whom to say no to. She has overcome quite enough obstacles and has skied through quite enough gates — though a few of them by the skin of her teeth. But she has never swept the board. She would rather retire beforehand, and return to obscurity with a knowing smile to the cheering crowds, back to the valley where a good soul waits to take her home unharmed . . ."

It is now almost eight years since I said these words. In the summer of 1980, as the whole world knows, Rosi and Christian began a new life together in the baroque church of St Anton in Garmisch-Partenkirchen — a life which they now share with their daughter Ameli. They must work very hard to maintain their relationship. Christian is not ashamed to be Rosi's agent — though of course he is far more than just that. And Rosi need not be reminded of the fact that her life with Christian would have been just the same if she hadn't won any medals at Innsbruck, and had simply stood at the edge of the *piste* and smiled warmly at some complete stranger. So any real doubts about the future happiness of the Mittermaier-Neureuther family are quite unfounded.

Victory at the Hahnenkamm slalom in Kitzbühel in 1979; Christian, Ingemar Stenmark and Phil Mahre

Rosi , Christian and Ameli

The magic of skiing

The word "ski" comes from the Norwegian word of the same meaning. The word can be traced back to the Old Norse word "skidh", meaning a piece of wood. This gives us a good idea of how skis were originally made — by splitting a log of wood. Not only does this sound primitive, but skis do indeed go back to prehistoric times. On the Scandinavian island of Rödöy near the Arctic Circle, rock paintings of a skier were discovered which can be traced back to a Lapp culture which existed between 2500 and 3000 BC. By 880 AD it can be proved that skiing was not only used as a means of self-propulsion but also indulged in as a form of sport. The Norsemen competed at "schussing" downhill. In 1060 we even read of Harald Hardrada racing in public against his rival Aslakson on a slope near Bergen in Norway. But it was not until very much later, in around 1850 in the area of Oslo, that competitive skiing began to take on its modern form. It was at this time that a form of sweeping turn known as the Telemark was developed, involving the transfer of weight from one ski to the other; and the first slalom competitions came into being. The sport of skiing has been known in Germany since the time of Turnvater Jahn. The Scandinavians had long been romping about on skis when the first German ski club was founded in Todtnau in the Black Forest in 1891. Soon after this, in 1900, the Feldberg became the location of the first German Ski Championships in the Nordic disciplines. From that time onwards, skiing became increasingly popular in Germany. By the 1960s, a sport which had at first been the preserve of a chosen few was to become a world-wide activity, involving millions of participants. All have been inspired by the enormous scope of a sport which never ceases to present them with new situations, challenges and experiences: cross country and mogul fields, powder snow and *firn*, slalom and downhill, and so on.

Skiing is a sport for all the family, whether young or old; and its communal nature is yet a further attraction. No wonder that around six million Germans have given themselves over to the sport.

But whoever thinks that the majority of skiers are from the mountain regions themselves is making a big mistake. Apart from Munich, Hamburg is the city with the largest number of ski clubs — which shows that the Germans are into skiing in a big way. Their numbers are for ever increasing, and their skills are for ever improving. Every year, more and more people are being seduced out onto the slopes by the magic of skiing.

Jumping over a crevasse — photographed by Willy Bogner

Piste, firn and deep snow:

Nowadays every winter resort will go out of its way to create the best possible runs for its skiers, and to provide the maximum enjoyment — from the first snowflakes of December right through to the spring. Every skier can find a run to suit his own particular level of skill, where he can let off steam safely and to his heart's content.

The easiest type of snow for skiing is the spring snow or *firn*. No other snow conditions can provide such effortless skiing. You feel as though your skiing were in a higher class. The bottom of a winding *piste* can often lead into a delightful *firn* slope, which no skier would want to miss.

The skier's dream is when a cold winter's day is followed by overnight snow. Now is the time for the most enjoyable sport of all: deep snow skiing. It is a magical experience, diving through the soft, shining, powdery snow in the glorious sunshine, wheeling and hovering down the slope in ecstatic weightlessness. Even falling becomes a pleasure!

Alpine racing is an experience which only a few can enjoy at first hand, but as a spectator sport it provides pleasure for millions. The skier is out there alone, competing for every hundredth of a second, giving a perfect performance amid the tense excitement of the race — what could be more stimulating?

Powder snow on the Weisshorn: the reward of many hours of climbing

Overleaf:
Downhill, the crowning glory of Alpine skiing: Canadian Ken Read races at Pontresina

Ski mountaineering is an exciting combination of skiing and mountaineering. As a sport it will always be confined to a small group of enthusiasts.

Ski touring and cross-country skiing are becoming ever more popular as an escape from the hurly-burly of modern life. The *pistes* are becoming overcrowded, and many skiers go out in search of the peace and tranquillity of the snow-covered mountains. There is something for everyone here: healthy, refreshing exercise; bracing mountain air; the enjoyment of shared experience; breathtaking views; unforgettable descents; and last but not least, marvellous material for photographers and cine-enthusiasts.

[Top] Ski touring near Arosa
[right] Arrival at a ski hut
[left] Stunt skiing in La Vallé Blanche

Helicopter skiing in Canada or the Alps is something which all skiers should experience at least once in their lives. Unfortunately, it is extremely expensive and very dependent on the weather. But thanks to the helicopter, even relatively unambitious skiers can enjoy an unforgettable experience which they will treasure always.

Freestyle skiing has in recent years been developed into a discipline in its own right, producing its own World Cup champions. Freestyle skiers demonstrate their acrobatic and aesthetic skill in the fields of aerials, ballet, and the mogul run. It requires a lot of courage and imagination to create what amounts to a dance on skis. However, all skiers will benefit from learning a few special tricks for use in awkward situations. The basic ballet techniques are quite safe and relatively easy to master, though shorter skis are essential for the purpose. However, stunts such as the double and triple somersault are the prerogative of a small number of specialists. Even some of the simpler jumps should be tried out first on a trampoline. Anyone who is especially interested in freestyle would do best to go to one of the various freestyle ski camps which are run by experts in this field.

Companionship: The company of like-minded people is undoubtedly one of the most popular and attractive

[top] Somersault on skis

[left] Helicopter skiing in the Canadian Rockies at the Mike Wiegele event

[right] Stunt skiing in a crevasse, photographed using a trampoline — a typical Willy Bogner trick!

aspects of skiing. Only a very few wish to go skiing alone. And even if you *are* alone you will soon get to know the other skiers — at the ski lift, on a tour, at the ski school, on the slope, at the ski hut or during the *après ski*. Wherever you go there are countless opportunities for making friends.

More than that, communal sport is an excellent way of bringing people together, and is vital to the development and maintenance of clubs and societies.

Anyone can take part, from the child to the old-age pensioner. And skiing covers such a broad field of activities that everyone can find at least something to enjoy. Thus all of us, from the beginner to the expert, belong to the one great family of skiers.

My relationship with the press

(as told by Rosi)

Innsbruck 1976, Winter Olympics: the first women's downhill event. "Rosi", they had said of me beforehand, "is a slalom skier rather than a downhiller."

Such had been the opinion of Munich journalists Franz-Hellmut and Ottmar when they had decided to watch the race on television from the comfort of their hotel beds rather than in the flesh. "After all, Rosi won't be exactly sensational, will she!" Even Harry Valérien, reporter for the German TV company ZDF, seems to have been rather doubtful of my abilities. I met him while practising just before the start. "Aren't you at the finish?" I asked him. "We're just about to start!"

"No," he laughed, "today it's the turn of the ARD [the other main German TV channel]. I'm not on until the day of *your* event — the slalom!"

"That's where you're wrong!" I replied. "You're going to miss something today!" At the time I rather wished I hadn't said that.

But in the event I was proved right. I got a gold! Harry couldn't believe his ears, while the two journalists in front of the television had the shock of their lives. "You fool!" muttered Ottmar to Franz-Hellmut as they sat there stunned. Still, both of them managed to produce an excellent report — and whenever we meet these days, we always remind ourselves of that rather amusing episode. There was yet another journalist who was involved in that victory in the downhill. Coming from Hamburg, he was not exactly an expert in the field of winter sports, but without knowing it he helped to boost my confidence. And this is how it happened:

During the training sessions my coaches never let me know that the other competitors were racing "all out". I at any rate had always tried to make the most of the upper stretches of the course, and it was only on the approach to the final slope that I had risen from the crouch position. "The others are saving their strength," said the trainers, "and they stand upright between each part of the course." And yet they were faster than me! Somehow I never quite believed this, because I could never think of a way of making up that time. So after one of my training runs I went up to said north German reporter and asked him what he thought of my competitors. "You know, Miss Rosi, you were the only one to stand up. Are you running out of power? The other ones are skiing in egg position right up to the last gate — everyone except you! Are you out of condition or something?" Inwardly I leapt for joy, for now at last I knew I was doing well . . .

I must say, I have always had an excellent relationship with the press; but of course there are always journalists and journalists. What about Patrick Lang, for instance? His father was Serge Lang who "invented" the World Cup, and he was the one who later at Innsbruck "kidnapped" me for the American TV, as Harry Valérien described earlier. But he could be a real pest. During the preparations for the 1973 World Championship in St Moritz, I was sitting in the famous Hanselmann Café with Christian and my chief trainer Kuno Messmann, when up came Patrick Lang to our table and brusquely told me he wanted to meet me that evening. I was speechless. "Patrick," said Kuno Messmann, "would you please go away?"

"Yes," Lang replied briefly "why?"
"Go away! Scram!" retorted Kuno.

I later became a kind of reporter myself. For example, I was one of the commentators for German television at the 1970 Winter Olympics at Lake Placid. Queen Silvia of Sweden was also present for the men's giant slalom, no doubt on account of Ingemar Stenmark. "You must interview her!" I was told.

The Queen was quite agreeable to the idea. I asked her, "Now we're both from Germany and we're both about the same age, but I've no idea how I'm supposed to address you. Please would you tell me? What is it — 'Your Majesty'?"

We agreed on "Queen Silvia" as the form of address, and the interview went ahead. But for some reason they cut out the part where I asked her that question. This resulted in a whole host of letters, mostly from middle-aged to elderly women, complaining that I had adopted much too informal an attitude towards the Queen.

Since then I have never had any more contact with the Queen of Sweden. Headlines have appeared in the press such as "Silvia to attend Rosi's wedding", or "Silvia to be godmother to Rosi's baby", or even "Rosi asks Silvia for advice about her baby", but these are no more than usual journalists' *blague*.

Our ski course

This ski course is full of technical advice, and has been divided up not only according to specific ability-groups but also according to particular interests and specialities. We have in fact divided the course according to the following international standard:
- beginners (L)
- intermediates (A)
- experts (S)
- individualists (I)

The sections for beginners and intermediates are primarily concerned with the basic skiing techniques. In each case they include, in addition to detailed descriptions, an example of a short and simple method of learning these techniques, which may be of assistance at these stages if you are teaching yourself. In the more advanced chapters — those for expert skiers — we have abandoned the didactic approach, and have simply tried to include as much information as possible about the sorts of techniques which are required on the ski slope. For skiers with a yen for Alpine racing, there is plenty of relevant and essential information in the chapters for intermediates and experts; but we have also devoted an entire chapter to the subject of Alpine racing, which gives specific advice about how to tackle the individual disciplines.

The content of our course is fully compatible with the official teaching plan of the German Ski School, which has gained more and more international prominence over recent years. Our course is not intended as a teaching plan in itself. Instead it seeks, by means of words and pictures, to convey a clear idea of those movements and techniques which will help you to improve your skill further and increase your enjoyment of the sport, particularly if you are teaching yourself.

Powder snow: a skier's dream

Classification into groups

Here is how the course has been divided up: mainly according to ability, but also according to interests. And here are some guidelines to help you. Like any true sportsman, you will no doubt be a fair judge of your own abilities and choose the group in which you are most at home. It is entirely up to you. Furthermore, a peep across the fence into some of the other groups will help you understand a little more, and will also give you a better perspective on the sport as a whole.

Beginners (L) — page 29
If you have just bought your first skis and you are raring to get going on those slopes, this is the group for you. Even if you already have some experience of skiing, but can only manage the very simple slopes with such techniques as ploughing, then you need have no misgivings about joining this group.

Intermediates (A) — page 39
If you can manage a shallow or moderately steep run with mostly parallel turns, or if you can master some of the more difficult slopes with the assistance of stem turns, then you are of intermediate standard. The aim of this section is the development of parallel swinging. We include some possible methods by which you can learn this.

Experts (S) — page 57
As the name implies, this chapter is not for someone who wishes to push a couple of skis around, but for the skier who has achieved full mastery of parallel techniques in all the most difficult conditions and situations. This section includes a number of different types of modern skiing technique which will enable you to widen and vary your repertoire.

Skiing in difficult terrain (I) — page 79
The word "individualist" is used to refer to those skiers who have a confident mastery of the sport and have a strong yearning to indulge in the more individual skiing disciplines such as deep snow and the like. In this section you will find a lot of detailed information about how to tackle difficult and sometimes unusual situations.

Tips for beginners

The first thing to bear in mind is that Alpine skiing is great fun. So don't be put off by any initial setbacks or difficulties you may encounter. You will very quickly master the basic techniques, and you will feel really pleased when you find you can already manage small descents without any problems. You should make the most of this feeling of achievement, because it will give you the motivation to go on to more intensive training and practice. In this respect, skiing is just like any other sport, in that it is the initial training which counts most — and remember this: champions are made, not born.

Movements which seem easy and relaxed in the hands of an expert skier are more often than not the product of continuous and concentrated practice.

However great your enjoyment and motivation, you should never overestimate your own abilities, as this will only serve to put your life and health in danger. A beginner with a knowledge of sport, such as a young skier with experience in other fields, can generally expect to make faster progress than someone with hardly any sports training at all. The initial stages of learning will be that much shorter. But given a little extra time and patience, even the most inexperienced sportsman will achieve the same in the end. The main aim of this chapter is to develop the *basic swing*. Not only will this enable you to make some quite decent descents,

but it will also form a solid basis for the further development of your skiing technique.

Equipment

Later on (page 91) we devote a whole chapter to the subject of equipment, which should provide you with sufficient information to fulfil your requirements. We shall confine

ourselves here to a few special tips for beginners. You will learn very much more easily if you have a special set of learner's skis of the correct size. However, as soon as you begin to make real progress you will often find that such skis will no longer stretch you enough. So it is best to hire a pair of learner's skis from a ski shop, and to wait until later before investing in a better pair of skis, which should then provide excellent service for a long time to come. As a beginner you should wear good snowproof clothes which allow for plenty of movement, and arms and legs should be well-protected against the inevitable falls. The boiler suit style is extremely fashionable at the moment, and it is without doubt one of the best and most comfortable forms of outer clothing.

Ski schools

Let us not misunderstand one another: we realise that basic theory can be learned and understood without the help of a teacher — but there can be problems here. We know that the insights which we hope to provide in this chapter are useful, but we also appreciate that theory is not easy to translate into practice. The learning process can be made very much simpler if you are taught by an experienced teacher. A good ski school will provide specially trained teachers who will show you how to do all the standard learning exercises and will always be on hand to point out your mistakes. If you have your children with you on your first skiing holiday, you would be well-advised to send them on a special children's skiing course. Not only will it mean you can enjoy a few hours' undisturbed skiing without them, but they will also benefit from the company of other children of their own age and learn from their example. So if you do not make very much progress on your own, do not hesitate to book a course at a ski school.

Getting used to the equipment

You probably had a chance to handle the equipment at the time that you bought and paid for it. If your favourite uncle decides to kit you out for skiing as a present, there is nothing wrong with this; but do make sure that the equipment is bought on the recommendation of a specialist ski shop. Before you actually go skiing, take the time to have a good look at the equipment — the skis, boots and whatever else — in the comfort of your home. Slip your feet into the rather strange ski boots, fastening them so that they fit firmly but without causing discomfort. Try to get used to the feel of modern ski boots — admittedly better suited to skiing than to walking. Now lay your skis parallel on the floor and step into the bindings. Make yourself familiar with the catch and release mechanisms, and practise getting in and out of them. You might try clumping around the house in your skis, if you are sure that the floors (and your new skis) will not come to any harm. Now take out the ski sticks. Pass your fingers through each leather strap from below, and then grip each stick so that the thumb lies on top of the loop. Adjust the loop so that you can hold the stick comfortably, even with thick gloves on.

By now you are probably raring to

get out in the snow. You may be able to find a suitable flat patch of snow in your garden or somewhere nearby which will give you a chance to get used to the feel of your skis in the snow. Lay the skis on the snow and step into the bindings, just as in the previous "dry run". Take care: the skis may be inclined to slip and slide, which is after all what they are supposed to do. Now start plodding around your little patch of snow, and try pushing a little with the sticks to produce a short slide. Try to coordinate your leg movements with those of the skis, rather as if they were

a pair of elongated shoes, and try to keep the skis parallel to stop them from getting tangled up with each other. When at last you do begin to slide, do not tremble like a jelly, but try using braking and accelerating movements. When you are accelerating, move the centre of gravity of your body forwards towards the tips of the skis; when you are braking, move it backwards towards the tails. You will probably be familiar with this technique from standing up in a train or a bus, and it is the basic method of controlling your acceleration while skiing.

Initial exercises

Let us assume you have arrived at the ski resort of your choice. Here are some simple exercises to try out your ability at moving on the snow. Seek out a well-prepared, even and gentle slope with a long flat run-out, so that you need not worry about how you are going to stop. Stand on the flat with your skis parallel, and try out the following exercises (star turns):

● Step round in a circle about the tips of the skis: stand on one ski, step sideways with the other ski while angling the tail outwards in a V-formation; place the first ski parallel to the second, and so on.

● Step round in a circle about the tails of the skis: this exercise is the same as the previous one, except that this time it is the tips that are fanned outwards.

Do not worry if you keep losing your balance by always standing on the same ski. Vary the exercise by stepping both clockwise and anticlockwise about the tips and tails of your skis, until you feel confident both ways. Now try walking on your skis: first in a straight line; then in a curve, by moving either the tips or the tails of the skis outwards. Continue this exercise until you have mastered it.

Now leave the flat area and climb the gentle slope for your first short run. Apart from the ski lift, there are two basic methods of climbing with skis:

● Side-stepping
Stand with your skis at right angles to the slope. Stand on the lower ski and lift the upper ski a little way uphill, keeping it parallel to the lower ski. Transfer your weight to the upper ski, then bring the lower

ski up parallel to it. By continually repeating this manoeuvre you will slowly but surely climb the hill.

● Herringbone climbing
Stand facing directly uphill, with the tips of the skis angled outwards in a V-formation. Step onto one ski and lift the other ski

[top] Star turn about the tips and the tails of the skis
[bottom] Side-stepping and herringbone

uphill parallel to its previous position. Repeat the manoeuvre with the other ski.

With both these methods you should place the sticks in such a way as to support your movements and prevent you sliding downhill.

Skiing for the first time

Now you have completed your first climb. Look for a suitable flat place for preparing for your first short run. Stand still with your skis pointing directly downhill, and try out the basic stance for straight running or "schussing". To do this observe the following:

● Stand with your skis parallel and not too close together — keeping your legs a few inches apart will help you keep your balance in these early stages.

● Balance your weight equally over both skis.

● Stand in a relaxed position, with your ankles, knees and hips bent slightly forward.

● Hold the sticks out from your sides at about hip level, but at the same time ensure that your shoulders and torso remain relaxed.

● Flex all your muscles a little, so that your posture remains firm but elastic. Do not allow yourself to tense up.

Looking deliberately in the direction in which you are about to move, push with your sticks and begin your first "straight run". Balance yourself carefully as you move, adjusting to the braking and accelerating effects of the slope. Carry on until you run out of speed on the flat. Climb back up the slope again and repeat the schuss several times.

As you run onto the flat again, try out a few skating steps with your skis (see illustration). These will increase your speed and lengthen the run. Push a little more strongly each time, with a pronounced forwards and upwards movement of the ski concerned.

Later, as you approach the end of a run, try a small step about the tails of the skis, just as you did in the star-turn exercise on the previous page. This will produce your first change of direction while actually skiing — a manoeuvre known as a *step turn*. As you continue to practise this, push harder with the ski on the outside of the bend, making the forwards-upwards movement more pronounced each time.

Even the most expert skiers use step turns when executing difficult turns. The thrusting movement which characterises both the skating steps and the step turns is indeed one of the basic elements of skiing generally. By practising step turns you are developing the basis of a technique which is both dynamic and stylish.

From snowploughing to snowplough turns

The next set of exercises will provide a simple and effective means of controlling your speed and will lead on to the development of turns and swings. The basic form for these exercises is the snowplough, and you should first try this out on the flat.

Starting with the schussing posture which you already know, move the tails of both your skis outwards. The tips of the skis should remain close together (but not crossing). You should keep the same flexible body posture as before, except for the knees, which are bent slightly forwards and turned inwards, pointing to the tips of the skis. As you do this

Step turn

Turning by means of a vigorous thrust from the outer ski

Alternating between the schuss and the snowplough

Skating step

A vigorous thrust from the left and right skis alternately

you will press naturally against the inner edges of the skis — a movement which will prove very important in the more advanced stages of skiing technique. Once you have mastered the snowplough position, you should try out the following exercises:

Schussing into a snowplough: Start the run in the schussing position, which will by now be familiar, and move the body into a more upright position. Lower the body suddenly into a more crouching position, while at the same time moving the skis into the snowplough. You will achieve this by pushing outwards hard with the heels. Take care that the tips of the skis remain close together. Continue to ski in the snowplough position, and be aware of the braking effect, which can be further increased by making the snowplough even more pronounced. Thus you can regulate the degree of braking by changing the width of the snowplough.

Varying the snowplough: Start the run in a very slight snowplough. Now crouch slightly while at the same time pushing the tails of the skis outwards with your heels, so as to produce a more pronounced snowplough. Now move upright again, allowing the tails to return to a less pronounced snowplough. Keep on doing this, extending the exercise into a rhythmical sequence of upward and downward movements.

Snowplough *wedeln*: Return to the very slight snowplough, and repeat the same rhythmical sequence as before. But each time you move downwards, turn out the right heel and then the left, moving first one ski and then the other into a more pronounced snowplough. By repeating this procedure quickly and rhythmically you will create the familiar "wagging" movement which is so characteristic of *wedeln*. The German word *wedeln* does in fact mean "to wag"

Snowplough turns: This time start in the normal snowplough position. Crouch slightly while pushing more against the right ski, and the skis will turn in a snowplough to the left. Move upright again while equalising the weight on both skis, and the skis will stop turning. As you move downwards for the second time, push more against the left ski: the skis will turn to the right, and so on. Make a mental note of this phenomenon, as it is one of the basic principles of skiing:

● Turns and swings always involve having extra weight against the ski which is to the outside of the turn.

Varying the snowplough

Snowplough wedeln

Snowplough turn

Traverse and side slip

We now go on to two further exercises which are essential for the development of modern skiing technique. The first of these is the *traverse*, which is to be used when you wish to descend diagonally rather than directly down the line of the slope. The same basic principles apply as for schussing. But you should observe the following new procedures:

● Stand more on the lower of the two skis.
● Move the upper ski slightly ahead of the lower ski by about half the length of a ski boot.
● Make the position of the body conform to that of the skis by moving the upper hip, shoulder and hand correspondingly forwards.

● Bend the knees slightly forwards and move the thighs inwards so that the skis grip the snow better and do not keep slipping downhill. This is known as *edging*.
● Bend the upper body slightly forwards and outwards so as to compensate for your edging and to keep the body balanced during the manoeuvre.

Try out the traverse position on a gentle slope. If you find you are going too fast, use the snowplough as a braking mechanism. The best way to do this is to crouch slightly while thrusting the tail of the lower ski downwards, thus skidding forwards in a sort of half-plough. This procedure is known as stem braking.

Rosi and Kuno produce a traverse by edging their skis, while Christian produces a side slip by straightening his body and placing his skis flat on the snow

The second of the two techniques is the *side slip*, which in the context of this course represents a further stage in the development away from snowploughing towards parallel skiing. First practise the side slip while stationary, and then while skiing gently. The manoeuvre will be easier to learn on a steeper slope. The technique involves the following procedures:

● Move upright from the traverse position while at the same time straightening the knees: the skis will move sideways down the slope.

If you wish to stop the side slip, edge your skis as before; this will bring you back to the traverse position.

The side slip will enable you to negotiate small steep stretches.

Stem turns

This turning technique combines several of the features we have already dealt with in this beginner's course. The stem turn consists of an alternate series of traverses and snowplough turns, and should be executed in the following way:

● Approach the turn in traverse position.
● Lowering your body slightly, turn out your heels, and hence the skis, and snowplough.
● Having reached the snowplough, put extra weight on the ski to the outside of the bend, just as you did for the snowplough turn. Your skis will move in a smooth curve in the snowplough position.
● When you have completed the turn, raise the body slightly and allow the skis to come together in a new traverse.

Practise the stem turn, going first to the left and then to the right. Then carry out a whole series of such stem

turns one after another. And when you have completed this, take a break from learning and enjoy a few small descents with stem turns.

From turns to swinging

Now that you have properly mastered the stem turn, it may have occurred to you that it takes a long time at the end of a turn if you merely allow the skis to come together into a traverse. Try accelerating the process by a deliberate movement of the inside ski at the end of the turn. When after a few tentative attempts you have made this movement into a positive one, you will notice that your inside ski will begin to skid parallel to the direction of the turn. Thus by the end of the stem turn you are beginning to move into a form of skiing technique which is known as

the *skidded turn* or *swing*. If you choose a relatively smooth *piste* for practising this exercise, it will greatly speed up the development of a stem turn with a swing-like finish.

The basic swing

The deliberate turning of the inside ski at the end of the stem turn is the first step on the way to the development of the basic swing, and we now intend to build on this. The basic swing is not only the first turn which will enable you to make much longer runs; it also forms the basis of a great number of more advanced techniques. These will be very much easier to learn if you have already achieved a confident mastery of the basic swing. Let us now go on to explain the basic swing: it begins in much the same way as the

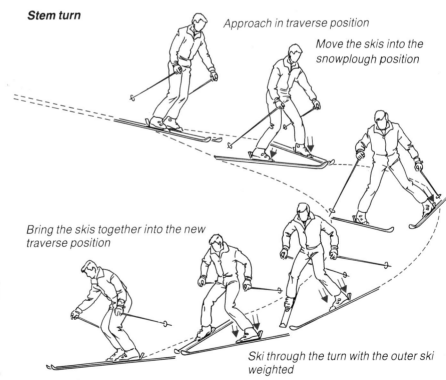

Stem turn

Approach in traverse position

Move the skis into the snowplough position

Bring the skis together into the new traverse position

Ski through the turn with the outer ski weighted

35

stem turn, but by the time you are facing down the fall line (the point during your turn when your skis are pointing directly downhill) the turn is already developing into a swing. The procedure can be described as follows:

● Approach the turn in upright traverse position.
● Lower the body slightly while turning out both heels, and hence both skis, into the snowplough.
● Having reached the snowplough, put extra weight on the ski to the outside of the turn, so that the skis turn towards the direction of the fall line in the snowplough position.
● Just before you reach the direction of the fall line, lower the body slightly and plant the stick on the inside of the turn (the details of stick planting will be dealt with later).
● Stop the lowering movement abruptly and immediately push vigorously with the inside ski. As you do this, quickly straighten the body while at the same time pushing with the inside stick which you have already planted.

While the body is upright, bring the inside ski parallel to the outside ski, which is by now heavily weighted and will remain so.

● As you bring the inside ski parallel, lower the body slightly while at the same time pushing with both heels to the outside of the bend. Also move the knees slightly forwards and into the bend. You will now turn with parallel skis in the direction of the swing.

● The upper body should be bent slightly forwards and sideways to balance the tails of the skis as they move to the outside of the bend.

At first you should concentrate on every individual movement or position. But with further practice you should gradually be able to blend the separate elements of the swing harmoniously into a single flowing movement.

Once you are confident at the basic swing — the first genuine swing of your skiing career — you can go on to try longer and more ambitious runs, making full use of the techniques you have learnt so far. Enjoy both the ready experience of skiing in the snow and the sense of achievement at having successfully completed the first part of our course.

It might be useful at this stage to consider one or two further details regarding the basic swing, the first of these being the use of the ski stick.

The planting of the inside stick is essential, not only to the basic swing, but to almost all the more advanced swinging techniques. The basic swing begins as the skis are brought out of the snowplough, and it is at this point that the stick becomes effective. The procedure is as follows:

The inside stick should be planted firmly to the side, between the tip of your ski and your boot, at an angle to the direction of travel.

● Flex the arm muscles and push while the stick is in the snow, with the hand pointing in the direction of travel.

● Remove the stick at the point where the upper arm becomes vertical.

If the stick is planted correctly it will help the skis to turn into the swing and provide a certain amount of support to help your balance.

There is another aspect of the basic swing which warrants more careful attention. This is the part where a vigorous push on the inside ski leads to the skis being brought together. It is in fact the most difficult part of the basic swing, and involves a principle which applies, at least in modified form, to a number of other techniques. The technique consists of two main elements:

Plant the ski stick to the side

Plant the stick as you move upright from the snowplough position . . .

. . . and thrust vigorously upwards to bring the skis together

● Lower the body and plant the stick preparatory to the manoeuvre. By suddenly rising from the crouching position you will increase the pressure between the skis and the snow, enabling the skis to grip harder and make the push more positive.

● Push on the inside ski and the stick as the body comes upright, so that the skis then turn parallel to the direction of the swing. The inside ski then becomes unweighted and is turned parallel to the weighted outer ski, thus leading into the swing phase.

Conditioning

(as told by Rosi)

A few years before Innsbruck, a journalist asked me, "Rosi, what is your opinion of physical training away from the *piste*?"

"Oh well," I replied, "when I'm at home on the Winklmoosalm and Dad wants a crate of beer, I go and fetch him one from the cellar — but I don't walk, I run. That's my form of physical training!"

I wasn't bluffing, either! it was the honest truth. For at that time I always used to say to myself, "Why should I knock myself out with cross-country runs and gymnastics? It's skiing that I'm interested in!" I had not realised that I would only achieve a consistently high performance if I was totally physically fit, and only then would I have the inner conviction of having done everything I could to win.

From a purely skiing point of view I had always been good: every winter produced at least one win, and that was enough for me — until one day I overheard a conversation between Christian and my father: "Oh Rosi — if she didn't for ever have other ideas in her head she could always be at the top. She's been skiing for such a long time now, but she hasn't pulled off anything really remarkable yet."

That annoyed me. But I became even more annoyed at an event at Badgastein, when an announcement came over the loudspeaker to the effect that Rosi, often known as the "granny of the World Cup", was waiting at the starting line. I was angry, but Heinz Mohr, our physical training expert, managed to channel that anger in the right direction. "Why only one win in a season?" he said. "With your ability you could get much better results and come top in every race!"

Those were just three small incidents — three little niggles — but they were to be followed by a big change of attitude on my part. From that moment — about 18 months before Innsbruck — the tide began to turn. And the Winter Olympics of 1976 were to be my greatest triumph.

There was only one way to achieve this, and that was one long grind of physical training. Previously I had trained with the team, which hadn't involved too much effort; but this was only because I didn't want to stand out too much — which would certainly have happened if I had gone off and trained on my own. (I had always been able to get away with this as my physical condition was naturally good.) But I no longer bothered about that. Heinz Mohr gave me an enormous amount of extra help. Fortunately nobody noticed this — as the team's top coach, Heinz had worked out individual training programmes for all of us — and so no one had any reason to object. Besides this, he often came to see me at home, so that we could go further into every small detail. My mother once interrupted us in the middle of one of these "home training sessions". The next item on the schedule consisted of three uphill runs. She was appalled at how gruelling these were, and wanted to send him packing. "You can do that sort of thing with the lads," she told him, "but never with my little girl."

The one who most enjoyed the runs was our little wire-haired dachshund Schnapsi, who would have stood a really good chance in the marathon in the Dachshund Olympics. What I most regret to this day were the hundreds of truffles

which we had to run past in the woods on our summer jogs. Heinz would never even consider stopping for them.

But then I suddenly began to notice; everything was becoming easier! Previously I had trained for what I had considered to be 100 per cent fitness — that is, what I needed then, not what I would need in the future — though it could in all honestly have been no more than 80 per cent. But now I aimed for 100 per cent plus — I thought of it as 120 per cent — and in the end I achieved that wonderful feeling which is a must for any sportsman, both physically and psychologically: that sense of being totally, and supremely fit.

Now I could channel this new-found strength into my skiing performance. And soon I was no longer a "flash in the pan" — I went on to become an Olympic champion.

For this I am very much indebted to Heinz Mohr. He it was who helped me to change my basic attitude and overcome the laziness which had always dogged me previously. But however much people are willing to help, one thing is true of anything in life: it's up to you in the end — and *you* must have the willpower.

Tips for the intermediate

Now you are no longer a beginner. You are one of the many skiers who can manage a swing with confidence, albeit with the help of a little stemming. If you have been through the beginner's course with us, you will by now be familiar with the basic terms. If you had already mastered the basic techniques and have just joined us at this point, you should soon find your way around. But it might be worth having a quick look at the last few pages up to the basic swing, just to check that you know all the basic terms.

The general aim of the intermediate's course is first to learn the parallel swing and then to develop some refinements of it involving "stepping". The first important stage in this process is the basic parallel swing — a much more advanced technique than any so far. Starting with the basic swing, we shall first introduce you to some variations of this involving downhill and uphill stemming, and then carry on systematically towards the parallel swing. Before long, *wedeln* will no longer be an impossible dream, and you will find yourself moving elegantly and rhythmically from one swing to the next.

However, it goes without saying that this course involves long and concentrated effort towards the development of technical expertise. Try to build up the necessary motivation and drive by imagining yourself as the perfect skier you want to become. And by hook or by crook you will get there.

Equipment

If you belong to the "intermediate" category, you should use skis marked "A" according to the international standard. Choose a ski length of about 10–15cm more than your height. By the time you have reached this stage, you will probably find skiing so enjoyable and fulfilling as a leisure activity that you would be well justified in investing in a pair of really good skis. If you are even more ambitious and are determined to become a really expert skier, you might consider buying a pair of skis in the "S"-category, which will prove extremely useful at a more advanced stage.

and quickly leads to fatigue. The movements involved in Alpine skiing can be divided into three types according to the three dimensions:

● Vertical movements: moving the body up or down.
● Forwards and backwards movements: movements along the line of travel.
● Sideways movements: to achieve the correct "cornering" or turning posture required for the swing.

Movement in skiing is primarily that of the legs: the upper body and arms are adjusted according to the basic leg position

Forwards and backwards movement depends for the most part on the angle of the ankles

Posture and movement

Continuous movement is the prerequisite for a natural, dynamic technique. Modern technique is no longer a matter of skiing in stiff, unbending positions, but one of continuous movement. Staying in one place for too long involves the muscles in unnecessary extra work

Vertical movements: These are normally produced by bending and extending the knee and ankle joints. Any bending or straightening of the body itself is less effective in vertical movements, as can be easily demonstrated, and neither do the arms need to be moved unnecessarily. You should therefore hold your sticks in a relaxed and natural fashion to the side of the body, whatever your vertical position.

Triple turns, showing angulation

Forwards/backwards movements:
To move your body forwards or backwards, move its centre of gravity towards either the tips or the tails of the skis, while at the same time keeping the body in the same basic relaxed posture. Forwards and backwards movements are primarily determined by the movement of the ankle joints. The shape of the hips, arms and upper body should be changed as little as possible.

'Cornering" posture (angulation):
The body must assume a specific "cornering" posture in order to obtain the correct balance while negotiating a swing. The exact posture will depend upon your speed, the radius of the swing and the amount of skidding in the turn. The rules for cornering are basically the same as those for traversing (see page 34), except that the body should be tilting inwards in the direction of the swing.

The basic criteria for angulation and cornering are:
● The outer ski carries more weight.
● The inner ski moves slightly forwards of the outer ski in the direction of travel. It is mostly unweighted, and parallel to the outer ski.
● The knees are moved slightly forwards and thighs and hips inwards into the direction of the swing.
● The uphill hip is advanced slightly so as to bring the hips in line with the feet.
● Similarly, the uphill shoulder is turned forwards, keeping the shoulders in line with the hips.
● The upper body is bent slightly forwards and outwards so as to balance the position of the thighs.
● The sticks are held in the normal fashion, conforming to the overall posture.

Perhaps that was too much to take in at one go. But only when you have mastered the correct cornering technique will you be able to produce successful swings. Your angulation must respond to the external conditions along the path of the swing. It should never become rigid, but should rather be continually adjusted throughout the swing as the conditions change. If the swing feels relaxed and sure, then your cornering is good. Every good skier — and that of course includes you — should work out his own individual cornering technique according to the criteria laid down above. And he should be continually improving it.

Negotiating a downturn

Forwards-downwards

Negotiating an upturn

Backwards-upwards

Negotiating bumps and hollows

As a skier, you must learn to cope with a whole variety of bumps, hollows and other terrain irregularities. (Probably you have already gathered this from your skiing experience so far!) Let us first consider the general principles. Bumps, hollows and ridges are infinite in their variety, but they can be classified according to a small set of simple criteria:

● Terrain forms which have an accelerating effect, such as:
  ○ skiing over an edge or ridge from a shallow slope to a steeper one
  ○ descending a bump
● Irregularities which have a braking effect, such as:
  ○ skiing from a steeper to a shallower slope
  ○ ascending a bump

Imagine the different irregularities you might find on the *piste* and consider the kind of effect they might have on your speed. Will they have a braking or an accelerating effect? Bearing this in mind, prepare to adjust your posture according to the following criteria:

● In cases of terrain which will accelerate, adjust your posture forwards and downwards to produce the appropriate balance.

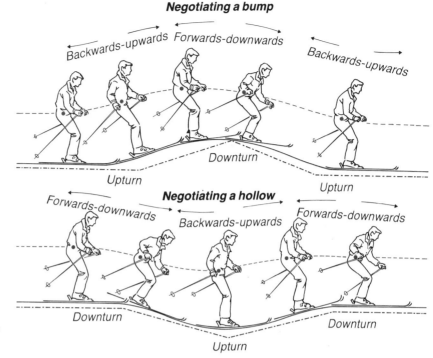

Negotiating a bump

Backwards-upwards Forwards-downwards Backwards-upwards

Downturn

Upturn Upturn

Negotiating a hollow

Forwards-downwards Backwards-upwards Forwards-downwards

Downturn Downturn

Upturn

● In cases of terrain with a braking effect, adjust your posture backwards and upwards, to enable you to compensate and remain in control.

These two movements should of course be further adjusted according to the prevailing conditions — your speed, the size of the irregularity, the general layout of the slope, and so on. Observe how the posture is adjusted in the four illustrations on the opposite page and above (downturn, upturn, bump and hollow). It is also important to ensure that the body's centre of gravity moves up and down as little as possible, however irregular the course. This can be achieved by adjusting the leg movements to compensate. You should try to use your legs like a combination of the springs and shock absorbers on a car. The principle of accommodating your posture to the terrain is not only vital for schussing, it also underlies many of the techniques involved in the execution of rhythmical skiing turns.

Further development of the basic swing

The first part of this intermediate's course has consisted of general advice. We now come to some actual skiing exercises which are specifically intended to develop your swing technique. Start with the basic swing and gradually introduce the following modifications:
● Shorten the snowplough phase: push off the inner ski and turn it parallel *before* you reach the fall line.
● Make the snowplough narrower.
● Emphasise the parallel swing phase of the basic swing by pushing hard and improving your angulation.

● Make full use of the stick by carefully planting it before you push.

The more effectively you carry out these modifications, the more smooth and dynamic the swing will become, however uneven it might have been initially.

We shall now move on to three specific varieties of the basic swing. They may well not come naturally to you. But if this is the case, then so much the better, since learning them will involve techniques which will come up again later on, in the development of step turns. These new types of swing will also lead directly towards our present goal: the development of the parallel swing. The basic techniques remain the same as before. The modifications apply only to the beginning of the swing — the phase during which the snowplough is used. The particular technique we shall use here is known as *stemming*.

Basic swing with downhill stem: In this particular form the name says it all. As you lower your body into the snowplough position, you should only angle the downhill ski. The rest of the swing is as before: stick planting, pushing off the inner ski, turning it parallel to the outer ski, cornering, and moving into the actual swing phase. Many skiers prefer this type of stemming: they feel safer and their skiing becomes correspondingly freer.

Basic swing with uphill stem: The opposite of the previous one, in that the snowplough is produced by angling the uphill ski only. The stemming is best achieved by slightly lifting the uphill ski and replacing it in the snowplough position. The rest of the swing is as before. This form can later be developed into a very useful step turn technique.

Basic swing with downhill stem

Upwards
Thrust from the downhill ski and ski stick

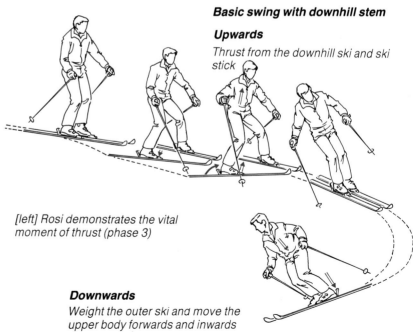

[left] Rosi demonstrates the vital moment of thrust (phase 3)

Downwards
Weight the outer ski and move the upper body forwards and inwards

Basic swing with parallel open stemming: This form of the basic swing leads us almost to the parallel swing itself. It cannot strictly be said to involve stemming, as the "stemming" no longer leads to the snowplough position but to an open parallel position. Open parallel stemming can be achieved using either the uphill or the downhill stemming technique. The

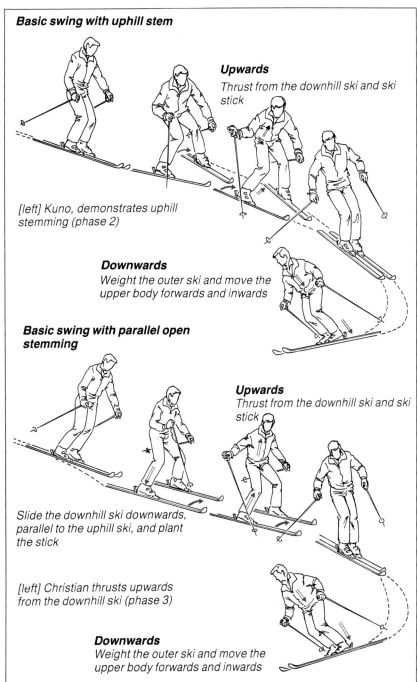

Basic swing with uphill stem

Upwards
Thrust from the downhill ski and ski stick

[left] Kuno, demonstrates uphill stemming (phase 2)

Downwards
Weight the outer ski and move the upper body forwards and inwards

Basic swing with parallel open stemming

Upwards
Thrust from the downhill ski and ski stick

Slide the downhill ski downwards, parallel to the uphill ski, and plant the stick

[left] Christian thrusts upwards from the downhill ski (phase 3)

Downwards
Weight the outer ski and move the upper body forwards and inwards

example which we use shows the usual downhill form of the open parallel stem. The rest of the swing is exactly as before.

Moving on to the parallel swing

If you have not had any problems in following the course so far, then the transition to the parallel swing should not present any great difficulties; you will already have mastered many of the techniques. We teach the parallel swing in two stages. If you are highly experienced in sport generally, then you might well be able to miss out the first stage. But if you want to be really sure of mastering the parallel swing, you are best advised to work carefully through both stages.

From the basic swing to the parallel swing: The development of the parallel swing involves just those techniques which we considered in the previous section: namely the basic swing with downhill stem, uphill stem and open parallel stem. You can now

A pronounced upwards movement causes the skis to lift off the snow

build on these by careful application of the following modifications:

● Gradually lessen the stem, bringing the skis both closer together and more parallel.
● At the same time modify your posture so that it becomes gradually more upright, eventually producing a noticeable upwards movement of the body.
● Start tilting into the turn as soon as the body moves upwards, thus modifying the upwards movement into an upwards-sideways movement.
● Make full use of the support provided by the inner ski stick as you approach the swing.

At first you will feel decidedly nervous and jittery as you try to enter the swing without the help of stemming. Indeed, at the beginning your parallel swings will probably still contain at least a hint of stemming.

Hopping as a preparation for the parallel swing: This is an important transitional stage towards the development of the parallel swing proper, and you should at least try it

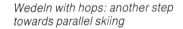

Wedeln with hops: another step towards parallel skiing

out. We have previously used stemming as a means of starting the turn, but this is now replaced by a hop into the new swing. The hop is produced by a sharp upwards extension of ankles and knees. Provided there is enough momentum, this will cause the skis to rise noticeably from the surface of the snow. The effect is further heightened if the manoeuvre is immediately preceded by a slight lowering movement while at the same time

planting the inside ski stick. The following exercises will enable you to familiarise yourself with the hopping technique and to take full advantage of it:

● *Hopping on the spot*
Lower the body, stopping the movement abruptly; plant the right stick; spring upwards — and the skis will lift off the ground. Land softly; lower the body, stopping abruptly; plant the left stick; spring upwards . . . and so on.

● *Hopping while skiing*
Find a reasonably gentle slope, and practise the same rhythmic sequence of exercises while gently skiing downhill. Take care not to lean backwards during these exercises.

● *Angled hops on the spot*
The aim of this exercise is to learn how to turn the skis during the hop from one traverse position to the opposite one. Hop on the spot from one traverse position to the other. You will find that you are pushing from the edges of the skis, and that swapping the traverse position will bring about an edge change each time you hop. You should plant the inside stick at the moment when you stop lowering the body, just as in the previous two exercises.

● *Wedeln with hops*
Try out the same technique while gently skiing, and you will produce a form of *wedeln* with hops. Practise this technique, each time deliberately moving the body forwards into the hop. This will make it very much easier to change from one set of edges to the other.

Parallel swing with hop

The hopping exercise will probably have made you very much out of breath. The reason we introduced it here was simply so that you could develop your edging technique as a preparation for the next exercise: the parallel swing with hop. The distinguishing feature of this technique is that the stem phase of the swing has now been completely replaced by a hop. It is during the hop that the edges of the skis are changed in preparation for the next swing. The hop is in fact an exaggerated form of the up-unweighting technique characteristic of a refined parallel swing. After the hop you should land gently with angulation, ready to enter the new swing. The swing itself will then be no different from the basic swings which we practised previously. This will be your first genuinely parallel swing, and will prove an effective technique, even in quite difficult conditions. Continue to practise the technique, and try to develop the hop into a natural part of the swing.

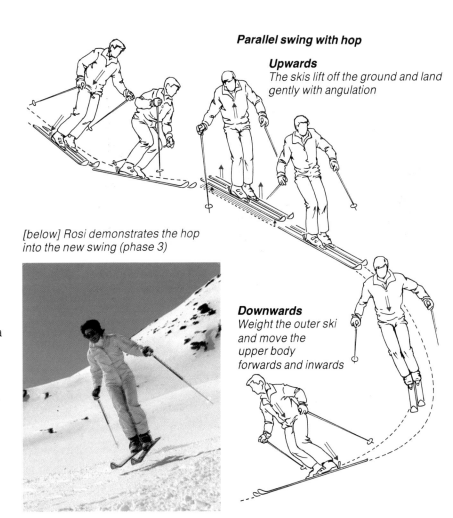

Parallel swing with hop

Upwards
The skis lift off the ground and land gently with angulation

Downwards
Weight the outer ski and move the upper body forwards and inwards

[below] Rosi demonstrates the hop into the new swing (phase 3)

Refinement of the parallel swing

The first aim of the intermediate course, as we have already explained, is the development of the parallel swing. You are already familiar with the rather crude hopping form of the parallel swing. We now intend to develop this into a more refined parallel technique by gradually reducing the hop. In the refined parallel swing, the skis remain constantly in contact with the snow. The edging and the leg tilting must still be changed as you enter the new swing, but this should be achieved without the skis ever leaving the surface of the snow. The hop is be a forwards-upwards-inwards movement. This will enable you to change the edges of the skis before entering the new swing.

● At the point where you stop lowering the body prior to the up-unweighting movement, firmly plant the inside stick. This will later assist the unweighted skis as they turn into the swing, and will also help you keep your balance during this vital but rather tricky phase which leads into the swing.

● The steeper the slope, the more pronounced the forwards-upwards-inwards movement should be as you travel into the swing.

should concentrate initially on the new up-unweighting technique which characterises the swing release. When you have gained more confidence at this, you should then start to concentrate on the swing proper and work towards improving that. You can tell if you have improved, because the skis will skid only slightly sideways as you begin to edge the skis more effectively throughout the swing. Once you have fully mastered the parallel swing, you will be able to say to yourself, "Now I can really ski!"

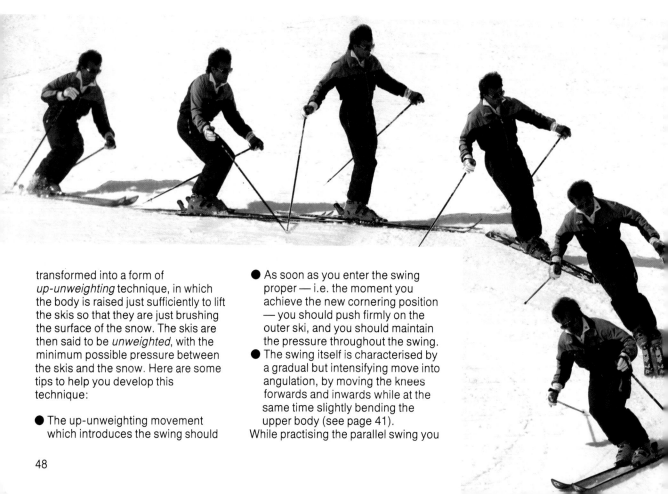

transformed into a form of *up-unweighting* technique, in which the body is raised just sufficiently to lift the skis so that they are just brushing the surface of the snow. The skis are then said to be *unweighted*, with the minimum possible pressure between the skis and the snow. Here are some tips to help you develop this technique:

● The up-unweighting movement which introduces the swing should

● As soon as you enter the swing proper — i.e. the moment you achieve the new cornering position — you should push firmly on the outer ski, and you should maintain the pressure throughout the swing.

● The swing itself is characterised by a gradual but intensifying move into angulation, by moving the knees forwards and inwards while at the same time slightly bending the upper body (see page 41).

While practising the parallel swing you

The principles of modern skiing technique

Now you have mastered the technique of parallel skiing. But before we go on to consider further techniques, let us stop to consider some of the basic principles of modern skiing. They are principles which apply to almost every technique or variant of it, forming, in fact, the essential basis to all modern skiing methods. The three principles are as follows:

- Pressure against the outer ski during the swing
- Vertical movement
- Weight transfer

The principle of pressure against the outer ski: In theory there are three ways of weighting the skis during the swing: Weighting both skis equally, weighting the inner ski, and weighting the outer ski. Weighting one ski only has a number of advantages, the most important of these being that it enables the skis to edge more effectively. This lessens the area of contact between the skis and the snow, thus increasing the pressure between them and improving the grip of the skis on the snow. This is vital, particularly on a hard, icy *piste* with very little grip. Thus during the swing it is always preferable to stand against just one ski rather than both. It is for reasons of balance that it is more sensible to stand against the outer ski rather than the inner ski. The negotiation of a swing involves considerable "cornering" skills, and it is only when the outer ski is weighted that the unweighted inner ski can be brought in to assist in case of momentary loss of balance. If during the swing you lose your balance for even a moment and all your weight is concentrated on the inner ski, there is simply no way of avoiding a fall. Note the following:

- Always put extra weight against the outer ski during the swing.
- At the same time put as little weight against the inner ski as possible.

The principle of vertical movement:

This principle covers all the many upwards and downwards movements of the body which we have dealt with so far. The basic swing is characterised by an upwards movement immediately following the point of thrust, while during the swing proper the body moves downwards as the heels are turned outwards relative to the swing. Vertical movement, and the avoidance of stiff, unbending postures, is vital to the development of a dynamic technique. There are two important aspects to vertical movement:

- *It should be natural*
  Because of the way our muscles are contructed, it is possible for them to sustain movement over a very long period, but they soon become exhausted if they are held in one position for even a short length of time. Vertical movement in skiing is thus very much in line with the way our muscles work. Even the simplest and most natural movements we make, namely

If you weight the outer ski accurately you should even be able to lift the inner ski slightly above the snow

49

walking and running, are brought about by the shortening and stretching of our leg muscles, and ultimately result in vertical movements.

● *It should be functional*
Vertical movement has a decisive influence on the complex interplay of forces which takes place between the skis and the snow, and upon which skiing itself depends. Up-unweighting prior to swing release will minimise the pressure between the skis and the snow, thus enabling them to turn into the swing; and the greater pressures which characterise the swing itself will improve the grip of the edges. The sharp interruption of a downward movement or the beginning of an upward movement will bring about an *increase* in pressure between the skis and the snow. Conversely, the beginning of a downward movement or the sharp interruption of an upward movement will bring about a *decrease* in pressure between the skis and the snow. This is known as *unweighting*.

Vertical movement is thus both natural and functional as a principle of modern skiing technique. It is an essential element of both the main categories of swing we have learnt so far: the basic swing and the parallel swing. Thus you will already be fully aware of the importance of building vertical movement into your technique:

● An upwards movement as the swing is released, so that the sudden interruption of this movement produces the necessary *unweighting* of the skis.
● A downwards movement during the swing itself, and thus during the steering of the swing, so that the sharp interruption of this movement

produces the necessary grip on the edges.

The pressure effect can be noticeably increased by a sharp interruption of a downwards movement immediately followed by a sudden upwards movement. Conversely, the sharp interruption of an upwards movement followed by a sudden downwards movement will make the unweighting effect more lengthy and pronounced. But quite apart from that, the effectiveness of vertical movement is also dependent upon the speed and direction, and hence the momentum, of the skier. If you work to build vertical movement into your technique, you will not only improve your pressure-control and unweighting techniques, but you will also bring a dynamic rhythm into your skiing, linking the swings together into a single harmonious whole. Learn to make full use of your vertical movement, and your skiing will become more effective, dynamic and confident — and ultimately more elegant.

The principle of weight transfer:
This particular principle has not so far been dealt with as such, though it has been implied in some of the exercises. But good weight-transfer technique is the hallmark of the expert skier, particularly in the field of Alpine racing. Some of the simple initial techniques, such as skating steps and stepping, will have involved a small amount of weight transfer. The principle can be defined as follows:

Christian demonstrates exaggerated vertical movement:
An upwards movement during swing release
A downwards movement during swing steering

● *Weight transfer* is the transfer of pressure from one ski to the other, such that one ski becomes weighted and the other unweighted.

The necessity for weight transfer is in fact a logical consequence of the principle of weighting the outer ski, since moving from one swing to another means that the inner ski becomes the outer one and vice versa. Weight transfer is thus an essential element of the swing release. It is also linked to the principle of vertical movement, in that weight transfer occurs in conjunction with the upward thrust which characterises the swing release. Weight transfer is again a very natural movement, being characteristic of simple actions such as walking or running. If the two principles of weight transfer and pressurising the outer ski are combined, this will produce a technique whereby both skis are working independently. Such a technique is both dynamic and effective, and is essential for Alpine racing. The elements which make up the weight-transfer technique can be described in the following manner:

● Press against the outer ski and lower the body as you leave the previous swing.
● Sharply stop the downwards movement and plant the inside stick in the usual fashion.
● Thrust off the weighted outer ski into an upwards movement.
● The upwards movement will have the unweighting effect with which you are already familiar.
● Now put your weight against what was previously the inner ski, which will be the outer ski in the new swing. This will complete the weight transfer.

In the case of most weight-transfer techniques, the edge change and the new angulation are relatively simple to achieve and form a natural part of the process. We shall now go on to consider a number of different weight-transfer techniques, all of which form a useful part of an intermediate skier's vocabulary. In fact many skiers feel more confident using weight transfer in a "step across" manner, with the result that their general skiing ability makes a noticeable improvement at this stage.

Stenmark: perfect weight transfer

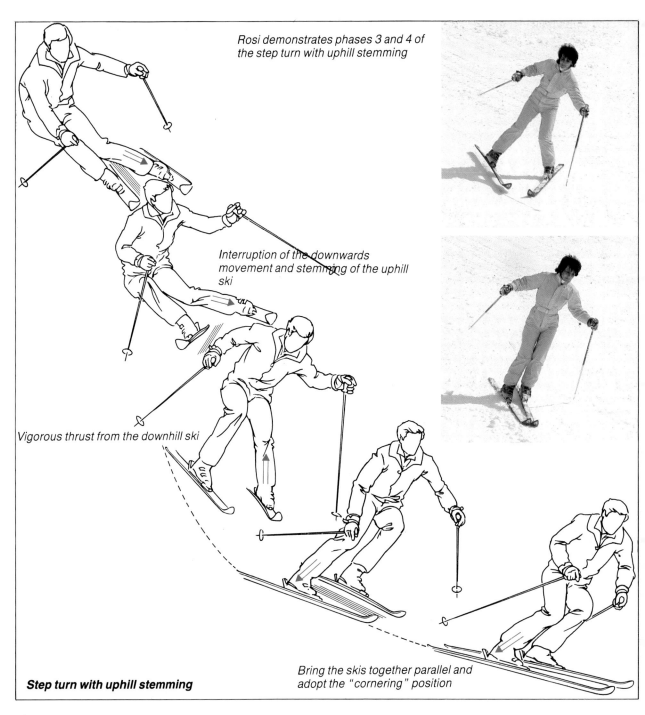

Rosi demonstrates phases 3 and 4 of the step turn with uphill stemming

Interruption of the downwards movement and stemming of the uphill ski

Vigorous thrust from the downhill ski

Bring the skis together parallel and adopt the "cornering" position

Step turn with uphill stemming

Step turns with uphill stemming

Think back to the basic swing with uphill stem (page 44). This earlier technique can now be combined with the weight-transfer techniques you have just learnt in which the skis are worked independently. The result is a form of "step across" with uphill stemming which should include the following features:

Steer through the swing with the outer ski weighted.

Stop the downwards movement at the end of the swing, while at the same time planting the stick and angling the unweighted inner ski uphill. Lean heavily on the stick if you wish.

Thrust the body upwards from the outer ski while fully stemming the unweighted uphill ski.

As soon as both skis are unweighted, step across to the uphill ski, then weight it more heavily as it becomes the outer ski in the new swing.

● Start "cornering" in the usual fashion, and steer through the new swing, putting extra pressure on the outer ski.

In this particular technique, the stemming makes the edge change both simple and natural as you begin the new swing. The use of a dynamic weight-transfer technique means that the skis are never used simultaneously but work independently of each other. This method is extremely effective, particularly in difficult conditions. Its use in racing has been demonstrated to perfection by the unforgettable Gustav Thöni, who has had great success with it.

Step turns with open parallel stemming

The difference between this technique and the previous one lies in the way

Step turn with open parallel stemming

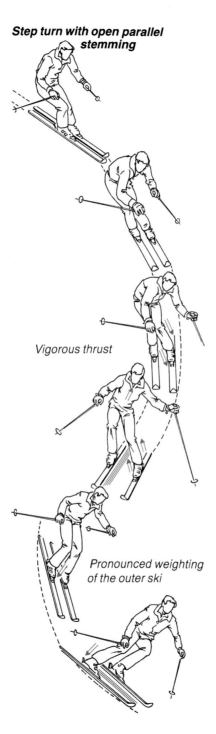

Vigorous thrust

Pronounced weighting of the outer ski

the unweighted ski is stemmed. This time you should move the unweighted inner ski uphill but parallel to the outer ski, and then thrust upwards from the outer ski. Once the weight transfer is completed, move the now unweighted downhill ski uphill, parallel to what has now become the outer ski. The rest of the swing is much the same as in the previous exercise. Note, however, that with this method the edge change can become much more difficult to execute, especially if the terrain is very steep. But the further uphill the ski is stepped, the clearer and more effective the edge change will be. The edge change can also be assisted by a pronounced forwards-upwards-inwards movement as you assume the new "cornering" position. This technique is particularly well suited to wide swings and high speeds.

Rosi demonstrates phase 3

Step turns with closed parallel skis

This exercise is much the same as the previous one, except that the unweighted inner ski no longer needs to be displaced sideways and remains in closed parallel position during weight transfer. The first part is the same as before. Heavily weight the outer ski at the end of the swing, stop lowering the body and thrust with the outer ski so that both skis become unweighted. As the unweighting effect diminishes, step against the previously unweighted inner ski, which in the new swing becomes the outer ski. In order to make the edge change more confident and effective, the up-unweighting thrust should be developed into a forwards-upwards-inwards movement. This causes the skis to become momentarily flat as they are unweighted, and you are able to move more quickly into the next turn. From a visual point of view this technique differs little from the basic parallel swing, the only difference being that the up-unweighting technique involves one ski rather than both. This

is just visible in the slight raising of the inner ski at the beginning of the swing. Given that there is no sideways movement of the skis, it is in some ways a rather passive form of weight-transfer technique. However, it is a very enjoyable method to use in free descents, and you will find that you use it more and more frequently as time goes on.

Compensation technique

The exception that proves the rule
In the last few pages we have given a clear and thorough explanation of the three most important principles of modern skiing: those of weight transfer, vertical movement and the pressure control of the outer ski. So it might seem rather strange to follow this immediately by confronting you with a technique which cuts right across at least one of these carefully formulated principles, namely that of vertical movement. Do the rules mean nothing then? No, the very fact that there are exceptions to these rules will if anything show how really important they are.

The point of departure for compensation technique is the existence of bumps and hollows on the *piste*. We have so far tended to assume that you have only had to deal with fairly smooth slopes, in which case vertical movement need only be considered in relation to a particular swing technique. And yet we know from the section on bumps and hollows (pages 42–43) that on an uneven *piste* vertical movement plays a vital role in compensation technique. At such times, when there are irregularities in the course, vertical movement is primarily needed to compensate for these, and can no longer be used simply to improve the mechanism of the swing. This means that swings on irregular terrain are an exception to the usual principle of vertical movement, and that vertical movement must here be employed first and foremost as a form of compensation technique.

Given that the execution of the swing can no longer be assisted by means of vertical movement, we must

Skiing over a mogul makes it easier to turn the skis

look to other methods of assistance. One such method is to adjust the route of the swings so that the irregularities in the course act in harmony with them and support them. Bumps in the course can assist the swing in the following ways:

- Skiing over a bump will tend to produce a momentary unweighting effect.
- As you pass over the top of the bump, only the midpoints of the skis will be in contact with the snow, which means that they can be more easily turned into the new swing.
- The shape of the bump will assist the necessary edge change as you move from one swing into the next.

Compensatory swings: Having dealt with some of the general principles, we shall now go on to consider how compensation technique can be used in practice to take full advantage of the bumps and ridges in the course. We already know that in such cases vertical movement is used primarily to compensate for the irregularities in the course, and that the bumps should be used to facilitate swing release. The compensatory swing should take the following form:

- As you approach the bump where you intend to begin the new swing, ski towards it in the usual manner, though in a more upright posture than normal.
- As you ascend the bump, you should first bend your knees, lowering your body relative to the ground, but keeping your centre of gravity level.
- If the lowering movement is not sufficient to compensate for the bump, then jerk your knees up in front of your body so as to compensate as much as you possibly can.
- Immediately before you reach the highest point of the bump, plant the stick firmly and deliberately.
- As you reach the point where only the midpoints of the skis are in contact with the snow, begin to turn into the new swing. The stick planting will be more effective in assisting the turn if the arm muscles are flexed.
- Once you have passed the top of the bump and the skis are edged along the course of the new swing, angulate and steer round the turn.
- On this occasion the swing phase proper coincides with the descent from the bump, and you should begin it by consciously stretching, or extending the legs downwards, to compensate for the descent and to ensure that the skis remain in contact with the ground. The swing should then be executed in a more upright posture than normal.

The hallmarks of the compensatory swing are a flexion/bending movement as the swing is released and a stretching/extension movement during the swing itself. The technique will prove extremely effective on moguled *pistes* and is also great fun to use.

Motivation

(as told by Christian)

If there is one thing I've had to learn in my skiing career, it is this: you will always ski better if you've done enough physical training during the summer and autumn — and to do this training you *have* to be sufficiently motivated. If you want to be successful, then motivation is everything.

In my own case I am forced to admit that I have never made full use of my potential. This can happen if things have always come easily to you — if you've always been considered talented and you can manage without having to try too hard. But unless the talent is complemented by 100 per cent motivation, you will never become a star like Ingemar Stenmark.

That reminds me of an incident with Ingemar which I shall never forget. The 1980 Winter Olympics at Lake Placid had finished with Ingemar winning his second gold in the final slalom. That evening at dusk, I was on my way to a small celebration party when I saw a man come struggling in from a long jogging session. It was none other than Ingemar.

I have another story about Ingemar. Once, after the long World Cup season of 1976, Ingemar arrived back from Canada in his home town of Tärneby, where he was due to be given a triumphal reception. But he avoided the crowds, and even though he was tired from the journey, he didn't go straight home. He drove straight to the local slalom slope, where he checked on the training possibilities for the following day. And this was

the end of March — and spring was at hand! But this is the stuff that real champions are made of . . .

My case was different. My first successes rather fell into my lap, and I was convinced I had the right attitude to the sport. When the failures followed, I blamed them on the equipment or the training, or simply on bad luck. I always had an excuse ready, and never even thought to blame myself. And my few successes encouraged me in this.

At the same time I enjoyed all the perks that competitive sport had to offer: the tours, the invitations, the autograph sessions, and all the various associated activities. It was a varied and interesting life, but it lacked the one element which is so necessary in competitive sport: the desire for total success — the desire to get the most out of the sport that one possibly could . . .

Not until 1978 did I see the light, though by then I was already turning into the ageing sportsman. It was Heinz Mohr, the same friend and coach who had brought about Rosi's success, who made me realise how

much I had wasted my talents, and who showed me what it was like to really live for the sport. And the logical consequence of this was that the successes at last began to come.

For this reason it has become my aim in life to get this point over to the up-and-coming young skiers of today, and the sooner the better. For the greatest experience of any sportsman is not sporting successes; it is personal achievement.

The coach plays a vital role in the development of a young athlete. At times he must be really hard on him if he is to put him on the right course for achievement. The right attitude and discipline cannot be expected to come naturally to youngsters. It involves a conviction and a determination which take a long time to develop. But all the really great skiers are basically self-motivated, and they find the necessary discipline and drive within themselves. When all is said and done, these are the same character traits which will guarantee success in every field of life.

Tips for the expert

Now that you are a really expert skier, we feel greatly honoured and flattered that you should come to us for yet more advice. You should by now be fully *au fait* with all the essential techniques; but skiing is much the same as everything else in life, in that there is always something new to learn. There is only one way to be really successful in sport — and that is to work hard and self-critically, and never to stop aiming for perfection. If you do this you will continue to make progress, which in turn will give you the motivation to keep on training hard. But at the same time remember that your equipment must also be kept up to scratch, and must sometimes be upgraded to keep pace with your skiing ability. Perfect skiing is the result of perfect technique matched by the best possible equipment. Moreover, however good your technique may be, it will only give you full control of the *piste* if it is perfectly geared to the prevailing conditions such as the angle of the slope, the snow conditions, and so on. As an expert your ultimate aim should always be to improve your technique, however good it may be already. Only then will you really be able to enjoy what you can do. Your abilities will improve most if they are backed by a healthy combination of sound theoretical knowledge and good practical experience.

Now that you belong to the expert category, you can emancipate yourself from rigid rules and learning methods. No longer need you rely on the slavish imitation of a given model; you should be concentrating first and foremost on the improvement of specific aspects of your own individual technique. Maybe you have always wanted to do it your own way . . . Well, now you have the chance to do just that: to develop a skiing style which is personal to you, and to explore it in all its aspects. But you should always remember that this should be based on a solid grounding in all the basic techniques which were covered in our intermediate's course, and without which you would never have got this far.

For reasons which have already been explained, this chapter is differently organised from the two previous chapters, which were intended as basic skiing courses. The didactic approach would not be appropriate; we can talk to one another as equals. We shall first

An expert should be in control of every situation

consider to what extent the material presented in this chapter can be related to what has been learnt so far. We shall then go on to discuss the importance of body and movement awareness in skiing. Such a concept is difficult to understand and even more difficult to describe. It might best be defined as a natural "instinct" which enables us to make the most effective use of our technique within a given situation. It is often said that "feeling" cannot be learnt: either you have it or you haven't. But this should not deter us from discussing the subject — firstly, because however difficult the concept may be to understand, it plays such an enormous role in the development of your skiing ability and skill, and secondly because we are quite sure you will be able to grasp what it is all about. We then go on to introduce some new techniques, most of which are merely variations of what you have already learnt. Finally, we offer some advice on the mechanisms of steering and swing release, which should provide the theoretical basis for some further practice in the improvement of your individual style and technique.

The significance of basic technique

In previous chapters we have tried to provide a solid grounding in the basic skiing techniques. Not only have we introduced you to a whole variety of swing techniques, but we have also given detailed consideration to the three main principles of modern skiing: pressure control of the outer ski, vertical movement and weight transfer. They are the building blocks of basic skiing technique, and they should not be forgotten now that you are an expert. But once you have mastered these basic techniques, you will have sufficient expertise to know when to bend the rules to your advantage. In case this sounds contradictory, let us illustrate it by

means of an example. We said that you should always press against the outer ski during the swing phase proper, and gave sound reasons for doing so. It would therefore seem logical that to put your weight on the inner ski is nothing less than a serious breach of principle. But if you are sufficiently expert to produce consistently successful swings while weighting the inner ski, there is no reason why you should not do so. Only remember this: if the result of such a manoeuvre is a wobbly swing which ends in a fall, then even for an expert it makes no sense to continue trying it. There are no limits to what an expert can do, provided it enables him to be in control of whatever situation he is in. That is not to say that the basic principles are no longer valid; on the contrary, it is the mastery of these basic principles which enables one to experiment. Unusual situations demand unusual answers, whatever the validity of the lessons already learned. In the exceptional situation where to weight the inner ski would save one from falling, it would be stupid to refrain from doing so, merely for the sake of the rules. On the other hand, it would be equally stupid always to weight the inner ski because of that one exception. You should never forget the basic rules but you should always be ready to break them if you have good reasons for doing so.

Objective situations and subjective goals

As an expert you should be able to free yourself from rigid rules as you seek to develop your full potential. But two things are essential if you are to achieve this:

● You must be able to make an objective assessment of the external problems and situations which present themselves — your equipment, the slope, the snow and

weather conditions, and so on — and to act upon them both swiftly and successfully.
● You must be sure of your own aims and intentions as to the form of skiing you wish to perfect — and then act upon them. If, for example, you want to go in for off-*piste* skiing, then you should develop your technique and buy your equipment accordingly.

The objective realities of the sport are mostly inalterable and affect us all equally. A steep or icy slope will not be shallower or less slippery for some than for others, as some would have us believe. Accept the situation, and solve the problem as best you can within the range of your own abilities. Your personal goals are of course another matter, and will depend very much on you. Some enjoy skiing for its own sake and merely want to become better at it; others want to win races; others again are only happy skiing off-*piste*. Decide what you yourself want out of the sport and plan accordingly, for only then will your skiing reach its full potential.

The "feel" for skiing

Every racing driver will tell you that he must drive, quite literally, by the seat of his pants in order to be fully aware of his vehicle and the way it performs. The racing driver must pay constant attention to the sensations he feels "through the seat of his pants", as they give him a vast amount of direct information about the behaviour of his vehicle. So too with skiing — except that the skier skis by the soles of his feet. The feet form a vital area of communication between the skier and his skis, and thus take on a particular significance in the field of *proprioception* or *body awareness*. Our feet — especially the soles — are covered with small pressure sensors which communicate detailed information via the nervous system about the pressure at each point and any changes in pressure which occur. The sum of all these sensations amounts to what is known as our tactile sense. We use this tactile information all the time, quite automatically and unconsciously, to keep our balance while standing, walking or running. Learn to attend to these sensations in your feet, and you will gradually become more consciously aware of them. They will eventually provide a continous flow of information which will help you to guide and correct your movements while skiing. The more you develop this tactile sense in your feet, the more accurately you will be able to adjust your technique to the changing circumstances. And the more practice you have at skiing "by the soles of your feet", the more automatic the information flow and the speedier your reactions will be. We shall now go on to see how this tactile sense functions in a number of typical skiing situations, and to consider how you might develop it to your own advantage.

Tactile sense when schussing:

Once you have become sufficiently sensitised to the tactile processes in your feet you will start to receive information about the various forces and pressures which are at work between your skis and the snow. When schussing, as we know, the skis should both be weighted equally, and each should be weighted symmetrically throughout its length. If our posture is good, we can sense this through the soles of the feet as they register equal pressure; the ball of the foot and the heel should also be equally weighted. The skis should not be edged while schussing, so there should be no pressure on the sides of the soles. Indeed, if you are schussing correctly, then the sensation of pressure should be concentrated on

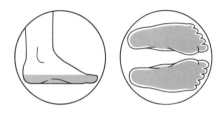

The pressure pattern when schussing in the neutral state

the middle part of the soles. First try to familiarise yourself with this feeling while standing still. Once you are skiing, the pressure pattern will be continually altered as you brake and accelerate and as the skis go over bumps and hollows; and this will modify the sensations in your feet. Learn to adjust your posture to these changes, so that the pressure always remains concentrated in the middle of the soles, whatever the external influences. Really good skiing relies on constant adjustment to every slight change in the tactile information which is received through the soles. The soles of the feet provide a constant flow of proprioceptive data which reflects the sum of all the forces and influences which are at work. It is your

job to interpret this data correctly, and to adjust your skiing accordingly.

Tactile sense when leaning forwards or backwards:

We have now familiarised ourselves with the tactile sensations which should normally accompany a good schussing posture. This state, in which the skis are weighted equally along their whole length, is known as the *neutral state*. It can be simply and clearly distinguished from both forwards and backwards states by means of the tactile sense. To remain in the forwards or backwards state is generally considered wrong from a skiing point of view, while the neutral state can be shown to be both safe and effective. It allows the skis to function more efficiently, and the skier is better placed to make swift adjustments either forwards or backwards.

The neutral state is thus defined as that state in which the pressure is equal along the soles of the feet, and it is the state we should always strive for as we adjust to the changes in pressure which we register in our feet. Forwards and backwards state lean and leverage can be recognised not only from changes in pressure in the soles of the feet, but also from pressures around the tops of the boots. Note the following:

● Forwards state:
  ○ increased pressure on the toes
  ○ increased pressure on the shins from the tops of the boots

● Backwards state:
  ○ increased pressure on the heels
  ○ increased pressure on the calves from the tops of the boots

The most obvious way of producing forwards and backwards states is by leaning the body forwards or backwards. But the equivalent effect can also be produced by dynamic changes such as braking or

● Weighting:
  ○ increased pressure across the whole area of the soles

● Unweighting:
  ○ a corresponding decrease in pressure across the soles of the feet

Tactile sense during the swing: By now you should be able to give a clear description of the tactile information received during the course of a swing. During the steering phase of the swing you will "corner" with good posture, controlling the edge of the outer ski and increasing the weighting towards the end of the swing. The correct adjustment to the steering mechanisms will be registered in the following way through the soles of the feet:

● Increased pressure in the middle area of the inside of the sole of the outer foot.
● This pressure should increase noticeably towards the end of the swing.

accelerating. Braking has the same effect as leaning forwards if the body position remains the same; acceleration has the same effect as leaning backwards. These effects can also be registered through the tactile senses.

Tactile sense when weighting or unweighting: We have so far dealt with changes in pressure which occur along the axis of travel (i.e. forwards and backwards). Let us now consider the effect of changes along the vertical axis.

Pressure changes along the vertical axis are produced by weighting and unweighting: for example, by moving the body upwards or downwards. But weighting and unweighting can also be brought about by dynamic changes: for example, skiing over a bump will have an unweighting effect, while skiing in and out of a hollow will tend to have a "weighting" effect. Weighting and unweighting can be sensed via the pressure sensors in the feet as follows:

The neutral state can be sensed from the pressure pattern along the feet

The degree of weighting or unweighting can be sensed from the amount of pressure on the feet

The forces and pressures exerted on the skis will change constantly throughout the swing. As you adjust to these changes, you should always aim towards a neutral position, superimposing this upon the standard pressure pattern of the swing as given here.

Educating your senses: Like everything else in life, the tactile sense has first to be trained. But even then it still needs further training so that not only are we fully aware of the information received from the pressure sensors in our feet, but our brain and muscles respond swiftly and automatically to carry out the physical adjustments which the information prescribes. The following suggestions may help:

● Your boots should fit snugly but not too tightly, and should not interfere with the transmission of forces between the body and the skis.
● Use insoles in your boots which are fitted to your own particular requirements, so as to ensure equal contact across the whole area of the soles.
● From the moment you put your skis on, make a conscious effort to be aware of the sensations in your feet. For example, you can try out the neutral state while going up on the ski lift, and learn to relate the feeling to that state.
● Ski fairly slowly on your first descents, so that you can react consciously to the information received from the pressure sensors in your feet.

By now you are probably sick of reading about tactile sense; but always remember that it is the cheapest and most reliable teacher you can have if your skiing technique, excellent though it may be already, is to be further consolidated and developed.

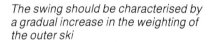

The swing should be characterised by a gradual increase in the weighting of the outer ski

Short swing with hops

Cast your mind back to the parallel swing with hop (page 47). In this exercise the turn was started by means of a hop phase. The sharp interruption of a lowering movement was followed by a sharp spring upwards which resulted in the skis lifting off the ground. The success of the so-called hop phase depends upon the size and the speed of execution of the vertical movements involved. Perhaps you have already tried the hopping form of the short

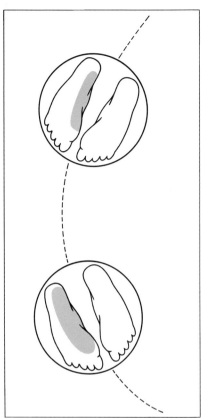

swing, by considerably shortening the radius of the corresponding form of the parallel swing. But you will no doubt remember the exercise in the intermediate's course which we called "*wedeln* with hops". The chief characteristics of this technique are:

● Turn started by means of a hop.
● Swing radius noticeably shortened.
● Swings linked together in a single rhythmic sequence.
● Pronounced vertical movement, including up-unweighting in the turn-initiation phase and a marked downwards movement in the steering phase.
● Vigorous use of the stick in order to maintain balance.

Turn initiation is greatly assisted, even during the hop, by the forwards-upwards-inwards movement characteristic of up-unweighting technique, which allows you to turn the skis more vigorously and to "corner" more quickly. The best way to perform the swings in the necessary rhythmic sequence is to execute regular swings of equal size and shape at a suitably constant speed, punctuating this by the vigorous planting of the stick. Vertical movement should be continuous and uninterrupted: you should gradually lower the body throughout the steering phase, moving directly into the up-unweighting movement of the new turn as soon as the old swing is finished. The short swing with hops, is a particularly effective technique when skiing on steep, narrow or difficult slopes. It is also ideal for dealing with hard and broken snow.

Refinement of short swings (*wedeln*)

From this stage it is but a short step to the more refined technique of *wedeln* proper. It has often been said that the mastery of *wedeln* is the hallmark of the true Alpine skier. The short swing with hops which we practised previously is really just a crude form of *wedeln*. In the more refined form, the skis are no longer lifted free of the snow, but remain in constant contact with the snow throughout the period in which they are unweighted. The basic form of the swing remains the same, the only difference being the more exact timing required for fine coordination of all the movements. The following detailed advice may be of help when learning and practising the art of *wedeln*:

The short swing with hops is characterised by pronounced and explosive vertical movement

- The edge change no longer takes place in mid-air, but with the skis in contact with the snow. You should therefore emphasise the forwards and inwards aspects of the forwards-upwards-inwards (up-unweighting) movement, so as to make the edge change more effective.
- Plant the stick vigorously, placing it further forwards and sideways than on previous occasions. This will assist balance.
- Delay the downwards movement in the steering phase of the swing, so that it is confined to the very end of the swing. This should then be followed immediately by up-unweighting and stick planting.
- On steeper slopes take particular care not to lean too far backwards, as this will adversely affect the rest of the swing. The best way to avoid this problem is to emphasise the forwards aspect of the forwards-upwards-inwards movement even more than ever.
- Ski rhythmically at a moderate speed.
- Above all, enjoy to the full that pleasurable sense of movement which *wedeln* cannot fail to provide.

Get a feeling for that sense of rhythm which is so typical of short swings, and which makes this technique so natural and effective. Practise switching from the wide curves of the parallel swing to a more rhythmic pattern of short swings: this is not as easy as it may sound. Once you have fully mastered short swings, you will be able to negotiate all the notoriously narrow and difficult spots with confidence and control — perfect *wedeln* technique will guarantee you unlimited pleasure and enjoyment of the sport.

Rosi demonstrates perfect wedeln: a combination of technique, rhythm, speed and the ability to take advantage of the terrain

Vertical movement in parallel swings

We have already spoken quite a lot about vertical movement in the context of swing, whether it be the downwards movement characteristic of the steering phase of the swing, or the upwards movement which characterises the start of the turn. The only exception to this rule is compensation technique, in which vertical movement is dedicated to the more important task of compensating for irregularities in the surface of the terrain.

We shall now consider in further detail how vertical movement is formed and developed as an element of technique. Vertical movement can be classified according to two main criteria:

● Range of movement.
● Intensity of movement.

By *range* is meant the physical limits of any movement which takes place, whether upwards or downwards. It would be worth your while to test out the maximum possible range of movement which lies within your scope, by first crouching down as low as you can and then stretching up as high as you can. The *intensity* of a movement, on the other hand, is measured in terms of the speed with which it is executed. In short swings with hop, for example, it is the high intensity of the short, sharp, explosive upwards movement which causes the skis to be lifted off the snow. The way in which vertical movement actually functions in practice depends on several factors: the techniques you decide to use, external circumstances, and the idiosyncrasies of your own individual style. There is one simple motto regarding the range and intensity of vertical movement: never use any more than you have to. You should always use just sufficient

vertical movement so that your skiing feels safe within the context of the chosen technique and the conditions. Here are two exercises to test out the range of vertical movement:

● Try out swings in an upright posture, alternating between a slightly bent position and one which is almost completely upright.
● Try out swings in a low posture, alternating between a position as low as you can go and one which is slightly less so.

Skiing in a relatively upright posture is more akin to walking in terms of the

range of movement required. It is more natural, and — since the leg muscles are more used to the types of work involved — it requires less effort. Skiing in a relatively low posture, on the other hand, makes for better balance, but requires considerably more effort, since the leg muscles must work that much harder merely to maintain the posture.

Rosi demonstrates vertical movement in a low body position, Kuno in a relatively upright position

64

Parallel swing with anticipation

The word "anticipation" speaks for itself: it refers to the anticipatory movement of the body prior to a particular manoeuvre. The start of a basic parallel swing can be usefully modified and improved by the addition of an element of anticipation. The process can be described as follows:

- At the end of the previous swing and immediately before up-unweighting, deliberately turn the body so that the uphill shoulder moves in the direction of travel.
- This causes the body to move noticeably forwards and sideways, and flexes the musles in anticipation.
- The up-unweighting movement immediately releases the extra tension in the muscles, with the result that the skis are turned more quickly into the new swing. To sum up, the muscles release the extra energy created by the twisting of the body, into the turning of the skis.

This rather exaggerated way of twisting the upper body at the end of the old swing can be said to anticipate the turn into the new swing, in that the position of the upper body thus corresponds to that of the rest of the body at a later stage in the swing. If you sense that the skis have turned more sharply than on previous occasions, then you will know that the technique has worked. Anticipation is a useful technique to employ in the sort of conditions which prevent the skis from turning, such as when the snow is deep or very wet. If your swings tend to veer off course so that they no longer follow the fall line, then the use of anticipation can help the skis to turn more effectively and bring the swings back into line. In racing — and in particular in the special slalom — there are a number of situations which can be dealt with far more effectively by means of anticipation techniques.

Here we have only talked about anticipation in the context of parallel swings, but it is a principle which can be applied to any number of other techniques, such as compensation or weight transfer — always with the aim of helping the skis to turn more effectively into the new swing.

Anticipation involves turning the body in a slightly exaggerated fashion, producing an additional flexing of the muscles

Down-unweighting

The most distinctive feature of this technique is that the movements involved are the opposite of those normally used in the parallel swing. The unweighting necessary for starting the trun is produced, not by up-unweighting as before, but by means of a sudden downwards movement of the body, appropriately known as *down-unweighting*. The steering phase is then characterised by a return to a more upright posture. Down-unweighting is in fact a further development of compensation technique (page 55), except that in this casc it is used on an even, regular slope. One might almost call it a variation on compensation technique. A swing with down-unweighting can be desscribed as follows:

● Drop the body suddenly in a forwards-downwards-inwards movement; as the skis become unweighted, begin to turn them into the direction of the new swing.
● Start cornering in the usual fashion, except that this time the body is already crouching down.
● Quickly extend your legs and bring your body upright, thus completing the turn into the new swing.

Down-unweighting can be used as yet another variation of swing technique, and for this reason it can claim to have a place among the many different forms of modern skiing technique. But if we were to develop this technique into one of the principles of modern skiing, it would clearly lead us nowhere. Down-unweighting is often very difficult to learn, even for quite experienced skiers. And to be perfectly frank, we ourselves simply do not like this particular technique. Besides, it is not absolutely essential to learn it in order to be an expert skier. But we try it out just once in a while. So why not at least have a go yourself?

Christian demonstrates phase 5

Down-unweighting

Lower the body as you begin to turn

Move upright as you adopt the "cornering" position

Jet movement

Given the way modern skis are constructed, it is possible to produce a very effective swing with the body leaning a long way backwards. Many of today's racers, the French in particular, have had great success using this technique. Jean Claude Killy made quite spectacular use of it, and celebrated a whole series of victories which made him the skiing idol of his time. The swing which has developed from this technique became known as the *jet* or *jet swing*, probably because of the way the tips of the skis often pointed up from the snow as the swing was started. The effect was produced by thrusting the lower legs forward at the moment of swing "release". The exaggerated backwards posture enabled the skis to be turned very much faster than might otherwise have been possible. Planting the stick well backwards helped to support the body as it leant backwards and made the turn even more pronounced at the point when the legs were thrust forward. This exaggerated movement of the legs is what is known as *jet movement* today. Like anticipation, jet movement can be combined with other techniques such as parallel skiing, compensation and weight transfer. In each case it causes the skis to turn very sharply into the swing. It is, however, essential to plant the stick firmly and well to the side, or else you will fail to produce the sharp turn which is required. The use of jet movement is extremely spectacular and can be great fun, but it requires considerable athletic ability. Like down-unweighting, it does not constitute one of the basic principles of skiing, but it is very useful to the expert in quite a number of situations. It can, for example, be of great assistance in very deep snow. Racers also make considerable use of jet movement, taking full advantage of its acceleration potential. On the next page we shall go on to consider how jet movement may be combined, first with basic parallel swings, and secondly with down-unweighting technique.

Parallel swing with jet movement

We assume you are by now fully *au fait* with the principles of parallel swinging. This time thrust the lower legs forward at the point when you begin to move upright towards the swing "release". Plant the inside stick firmly and well to the side, so that the skis can be turned sharply into the swing. If we compare this with classical parallel swinging, we can no longer really talk of a forwards-upwards-inwards movement, since the use of jet movement requires the body to be left behind when the feet move forwards. It is essential to start cornering quickly, and exaggerate your angulation, so as to neutralise the effect of the backwards position as you move into the swing. An exaggerated angulation and "lean in" will ensure that the body's centre of gravity moves through a very much shorter arc than the skis, allowing you to return to the necessary neutral state during the swing.

Down-unweighting with jet movement

The technique of down-unweighting can also be combined with jet movement by thrusting the lower legs forwards at the same moment that the body moves downwards. But in this case the legs must be thrust forwards even further — more than would ever be possible with an ordinary parallel swing. The result is a posture so extreme that it is only by firmly planting the stick well behind the skis that it is possible to maintain one's balance at all. But this combination of jet movement with down-unweighting is a particularly effective means of helping the skis to turn into the new swing. The body moves upright again during the steering phase of the swing, as in the original down-unweighting exercise (page

66). Start cornering early and try to exaggerate the angulation and "lean in" so as to neutralise the effect of the backwards state.

[above] Parallel swing with jet movement

[below] Down-unweighting with jet movement

"Pressure" turns

This is a technique which expert skiers often use without thinking when moving at high speeds. But the mechanism of the technique has been worked out only relatively recently. Like jet movement or anticipation, the "pressure" turn is an additional technique, and can be used in combination with other more basic techniques. Before going on to discuss the pressure turn in more detail, let us begin by trying to define it:

● A pressure turn occurs when the weighted ski is turned at the initiation of the swing.

Up to now, we have always tried to make the turning of the skis easier at the point of initiation by ensuring that both skis are fully unweighted. But a really good skier can also turn the skis

into the new swing while they are under pressure. You may ask if this is really necessary; after all, why should we go out of our way to make the skis more difficult to turn? The question is justified, but the answer is a fairly simple one. You can be a good Alpine skier without ever learning pressure turns — they are not essential to the sport. On the other hand, with pressure turns the skis are weighted throughout the swing, which means that the edging and control of the skis are both consistently good. This can be a big advantage when skiing at high speeds, when unweighting might easily lead to loss of control.

With pressure turns, vertical movement is no longer employed as an unweighting mechanism; on the contrary, it is used almost entirely for the purpose of controlling the pressure against the skis. We can demonstrate this by using the example of a parallel swing with

pressure on at the beginning of the turn:

● Lower the body as you approach the end of the old swing.
● As soon as you reach the end of the swing, stop moving downwards and immediately start to extend the leg, so as to achieve the maximum possible edge grip.
● This time, however, the upwards movement is not accompanied by the usual inwards movement, as it is not yet time for the edge change.
● Do not plant the stick until you are fully upright. At that point lean inwards to produce the edge change and "lean in" for the new swing. Edge change and swing release occur relatively late, and at a point when the skis are both weighted — hence *pressure turn*.
● Once you have achieved the appropriate "lean in" and angulation, start to lower the body as you steer through the swing.

You will have no doubt have realised on your very first attempt that the pressure turn requires a keen awareness of the principles of edge change and inward tilting. The advantage of the technique lies in the more effective edging, and hence the improved control of the skis. The skis are continually "weighted" as they are turned, even at the swing release phase, which means greater pressure on the edges and better control of the skis. It is for this very reason that racers have instinctively tended to rely on the mechanism of pressure turns. More than that, the upwards movement at the end of the swing ensures the maximum possible edge grip. This upwards movement no long assists directly in the process of swing release, but rather functions as a preparation for the downwards movement in the steering phase of the swing. In pressure turns, be careful

not to plant the stick at the point where you stop moving downwards at the end of the old swing; do so only when you are upright again and are ready to ski into the new swing. Pressure turns can also be combined with weight-transfer techniques (see page 53), whether with uphill stemming or with parallel skis.

Step turn with uphill scissor

This classic racing technique is very characteristic of the giant slalom. It is in fact a just variant of step turn technique (page 53). But you will quickly notice that it also relies on the pressure turn mechanism. We have therefore thought it appropriate to wait until now before introducing you to the crowning glory of skiing technique: skating step turns with uphill scissor. This highly advanced technique, which can also be used to great dynamic effect in freestyle skiing, can be described as follows:

● As you steer through the swing, weight the outer ski, as in all weight-transfer techniques.
● At the end of the swing, interrupt the downwards movement in the normal way. At the same time lift the inside ski very slightly into the air, giving just a hint of the scissor movement for which you are preparing.
● Immediately you have stopped moving downwards, give an explosive thrust against the heavily weighted outer ski, leading into an upwards movement.
● Immediately after this, displace the unweighted ski uphill in a scissor position by means of a *skating step*. You should by now have finished thrusting upwards with the outside ski.
● Weight transfer does not take place until now, and is introduced by planting the stick as soon as the

body is upright. Tilt the whole body and legs inwards so as to complete the weight transfer and establish the correct posture for the new swing.

It should be evident from this description that this technique involves a type of pressure turn. Firstly, the uphill scissor does not bring about an independent edge change in the same way as the uphill stem; and secondly, both skis are of necessity weighted immediately

following weight transfer. This skis must therefore be "weighted" as they are turned, which means none other than a pressure turn. For the same reason, the stick is not planted until the body is fully upright following the thrust, and only then is the new swing released. If you are skiing at high speeds or on a shallow slope, or if this is your first attempt at this technique, then it is better not to plant the stick; concentrate instead on making the weight transfer both accurate and

effective. This technique of step turn with uphill scissor can only be effective if the thrust serves to increase both the height and the speed. Practise the technique in the following way: execute two skating steps, both of them with uphill scissor, but only leading into the swing on the second of them. Take care to ensure that the outer ski is accurately edged at the point of thrust. If the thrust leads to a sideways skid of the outer ski, then it loses its effectiveness. The technique is well suited to swings with a wide radius, or those which veer away from the fall line. If you have ambitions as a racer, then this type of swing is one of the first essentials for your repertoire. The carving and control of the skis, the potential acceleration and the height advantage are all characteristics which will be of enormous assistance to the racer in passing both quickly and safely through the gates.

Improvements in turn initiation

Now that we have discussed a number of different types and variants of swing in considerable detail, we should like to consider some ways in which you might further improve your own individual technique. Any improvement will of course rely on the fine co-ordination of your body movements in taking account both of the continually changing conditions and of your own individual abilities. The advice which we give here is not specific to any particular swing or marking the beginning of swing release. The exact timing of each planting of the stick will ensure that the rhythm of the swings is both appropriate and well prepared. But stick planting is more than just a signal for swing release: the way in which it is carried out will have a decisive effect on the swing which follows.

You should normally place the stick to the side at a point between the boot and the tip of the ski, but the exact position should be skilfully adjusted according to the circumstances and what you intend to do in the next swing. Some useful tips:

● If the swing is to have a large radius, plant the stick close to the ski.
● If the swing is to have a short radius, plant the stick further away from the ski.
● If you are travelling at a relatively high speed, plant the stick further forwards towards the ski tip.
● If you are travelling slowly, plant the stick roughly level with the boot: very slowly, even further back.

technique, but rather applies to Alpine skiing generally. Given that most types of swing are distinguished by the form of swing release employed, we shall first consider ways in which the swing release may be further improved by the fine co-ordination of posture and movement.

Stick planting

Stick planting is the action which triggers off the new swing, thus

The sideways distance, as you have no doubt already noticed, will have a direct influence on the degree of turning which can be expected. The further sideways the stick is planted, the more sharply the skis will turn into the new swing. The better the muscle co-ordination between the skier and the stick as the stick is planted, the more effectively you will be able to control the turning of the skis. The more finely regulated the timing of the stick planting, the more accurately you will be able to adjust the swing release to the individual circumstances — and the more effective your technique will ultimately become.

Using the external forces
Skiing is characterised by the continual interplay of the various forces at work. Just so long as you can keep your balance and prevent yourself from falling, you will be holding these forces in check. But there are also ways of harnessing them and using them to your own advantage; it is these ways we shall consider here.

As you reach the end of the swing, you have no doubt often had the feeling of being dragged sideways down the slope, especially when it is very steep. You can counteract this effect by edging more sharply, heavily weighting the outer ski and bending the upper body forwards and outwards to compensate. Next time, during the swing release, however, you should stop trying to work against this sideways pull and give it free rein. The body will then move easily into the new swing. In the parallel swing, for example, you should simply allow yourself to be pulled into the new turn while at the same time deliberately straightening the body. The tighter the swing, the higher your speed and the steeper the slope, the stronger the effect will be. If you push too hard against this force as it tries to pull you downhill, your skis will begin to judder. If, however, you learn to take subtle advantage of it, the effect will no longer be to make the skis judder, but simply to nudge you into anticipating the new turn — which is of course exactly what you are aiming for. At first this trick may well go rather against the grain, but once you have learnt to take full advantage of it, it will save no end of effort and make the swing release much more confident. Indeed, it will often do all the work for you.

Christian takes advantage of external forces during swing release

Improvement of swing steering

The purpose of this section is to discuss the various ways in which you can use the fine co-ordination of movement and posture to improve the steering of the swing. Again, the advice we give is not confined to any particular type of swing, but rather applies to skiing techniques generally. The subject of swing steering warrants far more detailed consideration than we have given it up to now. We have so far only touched on it in the context of the different types and variants of swings. However, the better your skiing becomes, the more vital the steering will become; it is the key to further improvement. In racing, it is often the steering which makes all the difference between winning and losing in the technical events. Finally, we shall introduce a new method of steering which as an expert you ought to know.

The aims of steering technique
When we are considering improving our steering, we should be clear about what we are aiming for. A racer, for example, will have achieved optimal steering if the skis are fully edged and are never flattened at any point during the swing, thus minimising the braking effect. If, however, you are aiming to ski expertly merely for your own enjoyment, then your optimal steering will no longer depend upon saving thousandths of seconds. On the contrary, you will usually want to achieve a safe and controlled technique by means of carefully measured braking effects, so that control will be more important than speed. We can therefore divide steering technique into two main categories:

● Braking steering
● Gliding steering

We talk of braking steering if the skis

Above: gliding steering
Below: braking steering

brake more than the absolute minimum while turning, thereby becoming diagonal to the actual direction of travel. Gliding steering refers to those occasions when the braking has been reduced to an absolute minimum so that the skis are, to all intents and purposes, continuously pointing along the line of

travel. As you no doubt have a perfectly clear idea as to the kind of skiing you are aiming for, you should strive to achieve whichever type of steering is more suitable in your own particular case.

The criteria of steering technique
Now that you are aware of the fact that there are two main types of steering, let us go on to examine the different factors which determine whether steering is to be of the braking or the gliding variety. During the swing the skis turn about a pivot point, the position of which varies according to the way the skis are positioned at any particular moment. This pivot point will lie somewhere between the tips and the tails of the skis, depending on the manner in which the skis are turned. The rate at which the skis are turned can vary. This turning rate sometimes remains constant, but usually changes from one moment to the next. Thus the skis often turn more sharply, and hence faster, at the beginning and the end of the swing. Gliding steering is only possible if the skis are turned at a constant rate about a pivot point which remains at or near the mid-point of the skis throughout the swing. Conversely, braking steering results if the turning rate does not remain constant, or when the pivot point lies nearer to the tips or the tails of the skis.

Swing steering is dependent on swing release
Most things in life depend very much on what has gone before, and the same is true of the steering phase of the swing, where the technique used in *swing release* has a decisive effect on the type of steering used. The *swing release* controls the beginning of the turn, and to a certain extent determines both the turning rate and the position of the pivot point during

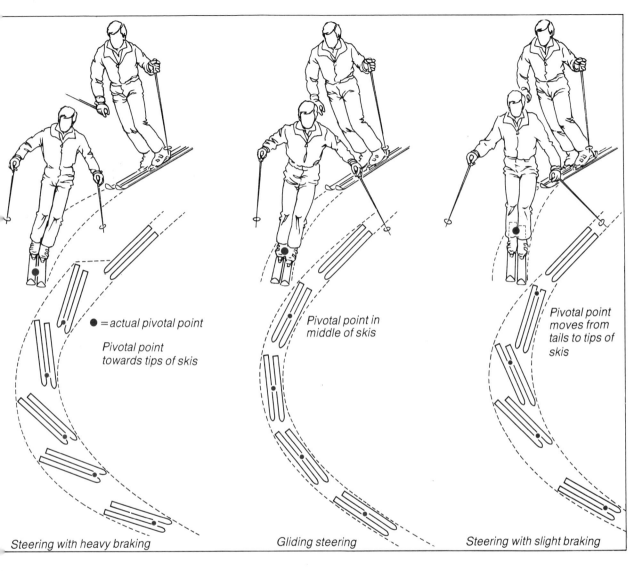

● = actual pivotal point

Pivotal point
towards tips of skis

Pivotal point in
middle of skis

Pivotal point
moves from
tails to tips of
skis

Steering with heavy braking

Gliding steering

Steering with slight braking

the steering phase of the swing. As we already know, it is the rate of turning and the position of the pivot point which determine whether the steering is to be of the gliding or the braking variety. The result of this is that the swing release and swing steering are inextricably bound up with one another.

If the swing steering is to be of the gliding variety, then the swing release must be prepared in the following manner:

● Your balance must be neutral at the point when the swing is released, so that the skis immediately begin to turn about their mid-point.

● The rate of turning must be carefully adjusted to suit the intended arc of the swing, so that it can then be kept constant throughout the swing.

If the swing steering is to be of the braking variety, then there are several ways of preparing the swing release, for instance:

- Lean the body further forwards so that the skis begin to turn about a point nearer the tips.
- Lean the body further backwards so that the skis begin to turn about a point nearer the tails.
- As you begin to turn the skis, choose a rate of turning which is either too fast or too slow for the actual swing you plan to take. Most skiers tend instinctively to choose too fast a turning speed so as to be sure of completing the swing safely.

As you can see, swing steering is determined by more than the timing and co-ordination of the body movements during the swing itself. You can in fact only improve on what has already been determined at the swing release.

Ways of modifying the steering
Quite apart from the swing release and the decisive effect it has on the rest of the swing, there are ways and means of actively modifying the steering during the swing itself, and these must always be used. The fact that you are firmly connected to your skis via the boots and bindings means that you can exert a direct influence on the behaviour of the skis. There are three ways in which you can do this. We shall take them in the order in which they are numbered in the picture above right, giving information about the effects they will have on the steering:

- Weighting the heels or unweighting the balls of the feet (1):
  - The tails of the skis become more heavily weighted, with the result that the pivot point lies near the tails.
  - The skis grip harder and steer more from the tails than the tips.

Steering in torsion position

- Weighting the balls of the feet or unweighting the heels (2):
  - The tips of the skis become more heavily weighted, with the result that the pivot point lies near the tips.
  - The skis grip harder and lead more from the tips than the tails.
- Turning the balls of the feet inwards or turning the heels outwards (3) by bending the knees forwards and inwards during the swing:
  - The pivot point lies near the tips of the skis.
  - The tails of the skis skid noticeably towards the outside of the bend.
  - The turning rate of the skis is increased during the swing.

Swing steering is a continuous process of regulation, compensation and adjustment, to ensure that the pivot point and the turning rate of the skis correspond throughout to what was intended, whether the steering be of the gliding or of the braking variety. After much practice you will become so expert that the process will become automatic, and it will seem as though the swing is steering itself. The results of telemetric measurement revealed that Rosi in particular preferred to steer using options (1) and (2). Option (3) of necessity produces considerable braking, and is usually the sign of an inexperienced, rather cautious skier.

Steering in torsion position

If, during the execution of a swing of whatever type, you twist the hips and the upper body in the opposite direction to the skis, this is known as *torsion*. If extreme, it might even be called *distortion*. Especially after you have passed through the fall line, the knees will bend forwards and inwards, while the hips and upper body turn outwards in the same direction as the skis. The upper body bends noticeably forwards and outwards. Steering in torsion position is both ,.atural and safe. It can be yet further improved in combination with the principles of pressure against the outer ski and vertical movement. The three basic

steering methods can also be quickly accommodated. However, exaggerated torsion leads to excessive braking, feels unnatural and places too much unnecessary strain on the spine.

Steering with body rotation

This is in effect the opposite of torsion, in that the body and the skis are turned in the same direction. We have deliberately not included this technique in our discussions so far, as it is only for the really expert skier. Skiing with rotation can quickly lead to serious mistakes, such as bad swing release, exaggerated weighting of the inner ski, and allowing the outer ski to slip away. But there are times when an expert can use it to great advantage, such as for producing wide swings in soft snow; and on such occasions rotation can be both effective and enjoyable. When you use rotation, your skis will tend to run flatter than with torsion. They will thus be easier to turn, but will tend to slip on a hard *piste*. However, exaggerated rotation is invariably wrong. As an expert skier you will soon find a balance somewhere between torsion and rotation which is suited to your own individual style.

Steering with body rotation

Egoism

(as told by Rosi)

What do you need as a person to succeed at skiing? A talent for skiing, the right attitude, self-confidence, nerves of steel, peak physical condition . . . Yes, all these, and more: honesty (towards oneself), egoism (towards others), the right equipment (for the particular type of snow), an element of luck (so that you reach your physical peak at the right moment), and the ability to concentrate.

For a long time I was completely hopeless at concentrating. I have even been known to turn up at the starting line with skis of different lengths, or with sticks that didn't match. But at least the weather was fine!

I went round giving advice to girls from other teams before the race, and for me the customary preview of the slalom course was no more than a quick run from top to bottom. During the race I would see old friends on the side of the course, which would set me thinking about what had happened in the meantime; and I would ask myself if I was the only one who had noticed the shaggy dog near gate number seven . . .

But one day, as I said before, I resolved to set my sights much higher — for the 1976 Winter Olympics. My attitude changed, and the winter before Innsbruck was the beginning of my "concentration period". I prepared myself thoroughly before the race; I no longer warned the foreign girls about the dangerous parts of the course; and as for team spirit, when it came to the race, I began to think only of myself. I know that sounds unsporting, but you must have a selfish streak in you if you are going to win. You should no longer be interested in whether or not the team are enjoying themselves, or that there's a party that night. I might even go so far as to say that having a steady boyfriend can be a handicap! If you are working hard on the *piste*, but all the time you are thinking how nice it would be to sit at home with your boyfriend, then your concentration vanishes.

But the marvellous thing about this change of attitude on my part was that skiing was just as enjoyable as it had always been — or if anything even more so, because now I was winning. And I still remained friends with all the other girls. The time I was most selfish was in the Olympic downhill at Innsbruck. I found during the training sessions that I could gain a lot of extra time by starting with a few skating steps. But I was afraid to practise this innovation openly for fear the others might copy me. The only person I confided in was my sister Evi.

Evi, however, was quite unable to take advantage of this. She was waiting at the start when she heard that I had effectively won. She wept for joy and completely lost all concentration. What is more, she cried so much during the race that she couldn't even see where she was going. A tragic situation, which I regret to this day. My own good fortune was Evi's bad luck.

But rather than end on a sad note, let me tell you about one of the funny things that happened. We were training for the Olympic slalom on a ski slope near Scharnitz, where the Innsbruck–Munich railway ran along at the bottom of the course. The news must have got around that we were training there, because we had no sooner finished our first run when one lonely railway locomotive came chugging along, only to stop dead at the bottom of the slope. The driver wound down the window and gave us a cheery wave. He watched us while we did two runs, and then suddenly took off back to Scharnitz. Barely five minutes had gone by when the Munich express came thundering past. Another five minutes and the loco came chugging back . . .

Next day Klaus Mayr planned our schedule according to the train timetable. We trained from ten till twelve in the morning, because at that time there were no trains on the Scharnitz stretch of the line!

Heidi, Rosi and Evi Mittermaier

Tips for skiing in difficult terrain

Skiing is fascinating for all of us, simply because of the new challenges and situation which it presents to us each day. Everything is constantly changing: the slope, the light, the temperature, the height, our speed and physical condition, or the number of skiers around us.

What is more, the snow we enjoy so much is so sensitive to these changes that the conditions at the top of the slope can be entirely different from those at the bottom.

It will be clear from this that our chief problem is that of adjusting to the wide fluctuations in the condition of the snow and of the *piste*. We may be fully *au fait* with all the basic techniques, but that is really only half the battle. We also have to learn how to find the right technique for each individual situation.

In this chapter we shall go into more detail about some of the more extreme situations which the Alpine skier might meet, and offer some suggestions as to how they might safely be overcome.

Deep snow skiing

Skiing away from the *piste* can be one of the most satisfying experiences of all. It must surely be every skier's dream to lay the first tracks in a field of fresh virgin snow! An expert skier can easily become addicted, and will be for ever lured away from the *piste* into unexplored terrain.

We believe every skier should have

the chance to savour this magical experience. So here are a few tips and suggestions:

- Ski as near to the fall line as possible before making your first swing. This will help you to build up speed, and you will not need to turn the skis so much. Wait until you have got into the rhythm before moving into larger swings.
- When skiing off the *piste* for the first time, it is all too easy to fall through skiing too slowly. It is therefore important to pluck up the courage to ski fast.
- Try to find a steep or at least moderately steep slope, as this will help to overcome the resistance between the skis and the deep snow.
- Off-*piste* skiing is very tiring for the beginner, so try it out first on a slope not far from the *piste*. Then if you are in danger of exhaustion you can quickly get back to the *piste*, where the going is less tiring.
- Take care to keep the skis fairly close together, and avoid any sudden changes in the weighting of the skis.
- Always weight the skis as equally as possible.
- The more you weight one ski at the expense of the other, the more it will bury itself in the snow, while the unweighted ski will tend to run away from you.
- Try to swing as rhythmically and as near to the fall line as possible.
- Parallel *wedeln* (page 64) is the most effective and enjoyable technique to use in powder snow, as it enables you to stay close to the fall line and keep a regular rhythm. You should also emphasise the vertical movement.
- When skiing in deep snow you can, or rather should, exaggerate your inward lean, so as to counteract the increased resistance of the snow.

Skiing through a thin layer of powder snow

Powder snow

Firm snow

Ground

If the powder is only thin, ski as you would normally do on the piste

Skiing through deep powder snow

Powder snow

Firm snow

Ground

If the powder is deep, adjust your body posture backwards so as to keep the ski tips above the surface of the snow

- Always stand on the heels when skiing through deep snow, so that the ski tips stay above the surface and do not bore into the snow. The extent to which you do this should be gauged carefully according to the depth of the snow.
- The ideal technique for use in deep or moderately deep powder snow is jet movement combined with up-unweighting or down-unweighting (see page 68). The forwards thrust of the feet helps the ski tips to mount the surface of the snow.

Skiing in powder snow

Lean slightly backwards as you lower your body, pushing your thighs slightly forwards in a jet movement

Lean inwards as you straighten your body and turn the skis

Turn immediately into the next swing

Skiing off-piste in the Canadian Rockies

Special equipment

If you want to buy special skis for skiing in deep snow, then they should be somewhat shorter and a little broader than usual. They should also be soft and malleable towards the tips.

Avoid using ski brakes when skiing in deep snow. If you fall, the skis will tend to come off and bury themselves in the snow, and you may lose them for good. The Canadians, who are the real experts in deep snow, prefer to use five-foot-long red straps of some lightweight material which they attach to the heel bindings. These are so light that they always stay above the snow, making it much easier to locate a buried ski.

Moguled piste

Moguled *pistes* are not exactly easy to deal with, and they occur mostly on steep slopes. But they are marvellous places for experts to show off their technique, because they offer such a wide variety of terrain. The most important thing is to make the moguls work *for* you rather than *against* you. Try to organise your route through the moguls so as to produce a sequence of swings which is both rhythmic and dynamic.

There are three main ways of dealing with a moguled *piste*:

1. Skiing *over* the moguls
2. Skiing *round* the moguls
3. Skiing *through* the moguls (a combination of 1 and 2)

● Before you begin, decide roughly what route you are going to follow.
● The secret of good mogul skiing is always to anticipate as far ahead as possible.
● The best way to swing *over* the moguls is by means of compensation technique (page 55). This method will pose no great problems, even at a slow speed, since the skis can be quickly and easily turned at the top of the bump.
● Parallel swinging and weight transfer are the best techniques for skiing *round* the bump. This method requires less compensation, and is therefore better for skiing at high speeds.
● Swinging *through* the moguls is the method most frequently used. To do it you must be ready to use every technique you have learnt. The first essential is for the body to be flexible and relaxed, so as to absorb every bump or hollow in the course; and you should never lose contact with the ground.

Skiing over the moguls

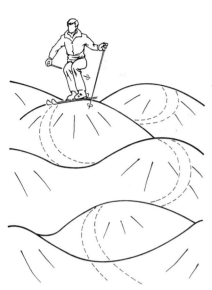

Release the swing at the top of the mogul, preferably with the help of compensation technique

Steer through the swing as you move down into the hollow

Skiing round the moguls

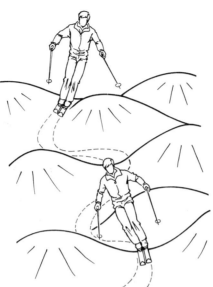

Release the swing in the hollow, preferably with the help of weight-transfer technique

Continue along the hollow as you steer through the swing

Skiing through the moguls

The route is determined by the skier and not by the terrain; it requires good eyesight and reactions and a versatile technique

● If you are really expert you might occasionally try jumping over a mogul, particularly if it has sharp edges. Provided that the jump is both gentle and controlled, you will have no trouble in keeping your body under control.

During the time that we were racing, we always had regular sessions on a moguled *piste*. This helped to keep us relaxed and supple after the somewhat one-sided training which we had to do. It was always a challenge, but it was great fun too. And it will always be fun for as long as we continue to ski.

Ice and hard-frozen snow

The courses we had to race on were more often than not covered in a thick layer of ice, so we were used to coping with such extreme conditions. But we still try to steer clear of icy *pistes* if at all possible. You must know how to deal with them when you must ski them, though, so here are some tips:

- Keep the skis well edged.
- Fasten your boots tighter.
- Control your skiing carefully; keep the skis wider apart than usual, while leaning the body forwards and outwards so as to put even more weight on the downhill ski.
- The best technique to use is the short swing with hops (page 61). Then push briefly but explosively on the edges of the skis as you move into the hop which initiates the swing. Plant the downhill stick vigorously so as to give full support to the turn. Turn the skis round completely with every swing so as to avoid going too fast. As you approach the end of the swing, try to concentrate the edge pressure towards the tails of the skis by flexing the knees forwards and inwards.
- Ski as near to the edge of the *piste* as you can: you will usually find there is less ice in this area.
- You will sometimes find enormous sheets of ice ending in irregular areas of granular snow. Keep a sharp eye out for these. Ski as straight as you can across the ice, and prepare to swing as soon as you meet the snow.
- Keep your distance from obstacles and from other skiers.

Leg-breaker snow

Crusted snow

Crusted snow is most often found beyond the edges of the *piste*. It is characterised by a hard, crusted surface, which has a nasty habit of breaking under the weight of the skier. This sort of situation crops up all too often at the foot of a marvellous *firn* slope. If you are lucky the crust will just hold your weight, in which case here are some tips:

- Try to make yourself as light as possible.
- Avoid sudden movements or changes in weighting.
- Weight both skis equally.
- Keep the skis as flat as possible.
- Ski slowly in broad swings, edging the skis as little as possible.

If you are unlucky, the snow crust will break down under your weight, and it will become almost impossible to turn the skis. Such situations make enormous demands on both technique and fitness:

- Ski with conviction, summoning up all the strength you can.
- The safest and most energy-saving method is a traverse followed by a kick turn. This is also the best method for less experienced skiers.
- The expert skier will be able to replace the kick turn by a kind of hopping turn, in which the skier hops from one traverse to the next by pushing vigorously on both sticks and turning the skis in mid air. Skiers often make the mistake of not pushing hard enough on the sticks or of traversing too fast before the turn.
- If you are an expert, you can also try using short swings with hops (page 61). We find that we cannot keep this up for very long, as it is incredibly exhausting. In fact it is quite a relief to go back to traversing.
- One very effective method of lessening your speed is to use a few step turns. Make several sideways steps with the uphill ski, each time bringing the downhill ski up afterwards.

This picture shows the typical track which Christian leaves as he hops through crusted snow

Christian works hard to hop down a heavily crusted slope — the only situation in which such large hops are recommended

Soft *firn* or heavy, slushy snow

These are types of snow in which the skis sink in deep and are prevented from turning by the resistance of the snow. You should therefore use techniques similar to those used in broken, crusted snow (see the previous page). But there is nothing to prevent you using the good old-fashioned step turn in such circumstances.

Wet and sticky snow

These unpleasant conditions are often found when the *piste* is covered by a thin layer of new and rather wet snow. The new snow tends to drag on the skis, forcing the body to bend forward, and sometimes almost pulling your boots off. A sudden return to the old snow surface will cause your skis to accelerate and you to lean back suddenly.

- Be sure to wax your skis well. A little paraffin wax rubbed directly into the base will work wonders.
- Ski as close to the fall line as possible.
- Take care to remain in neutral balance (page 59), so that you are ready to adjust quickly to any sudden braking or accelerating effects, thus preventing you from falling.

Steep slopes and precipices

Speed control is the first essential when skiing down steep slopes.

- Avoid schussing, even for short runs.
- If you feel unsafe, side slip.

- Begin your swings by swinging slightly in the opposite direction, or by using the braking effect of downhill stemming.
- Tight swings with sharp turns are best.
- Put extra weight against the outer ski and exaggerate your hip angulation.
- Short swings are the preferred technique. Place the skis as nearly horizontal as possible. After the thrust, turn the skis as quickly as possible into the new position so that you can brake effectively.
- It is vital to push hard on the downhill stick in order to be able to turn and brake effectively.
- Never lean into the turn, however hard it may seem not to do so.
- If you fall, try to turn the skis below you and across the fall line, so that the edges can be used as a brake.

High speeds

Skiing at high speeds is one of the most challenging aspects of the sport. Not for nothing is the downhill the most popular Alpine spectator sport.

Most skiers enjoy skiing fast. We for our own part simply adore it. Note, however, that skiing at speed requires more than just courage and stamina: it demands considerable technical ability and knowhow. You should also bear in mind that in a race a racer always skis alone on a specially prepared *piste*, and has been specifically trained and qualified for skiing at high speeds. Skiing at high speeds on a public *piste* requires considerable care and a very responsible attitude. Note the following points:

- As you ski faster, you should increase your safety margins accordingly, and allow for a greater braking distance.
- Look well ahead.
- Take note of even the slightest irregularity in the terrain.
- Always try to remain in neutral balance so as to be ready to compensate for bumps and moguls.
- Keep your hands in front of you and your body relaxed.
- Keep your skis just over a foot apart.

- Never lean too far back.
- Always have a quick look up the slope when you brake: some people will be even faster than you!
- The most effective way of stopping is the emergency stop (page 88).
- If you suddenly run into moguls at high speed, it will be very difficult to compensate sufficiently. In order to avoid falling, it would be sensible at the very least to hop over the large moguls.

Emergency stop

Unfortunately skis do not have any brakes, and yet it is just as important for the skier as for the driver to be able to brake quickly and effectively. You have no doubt seen downhill racers brake sharply and successfully from enormous speeds as they reach the finish. They are in fact using a

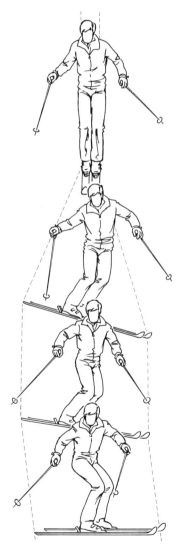

Rosi uses an emergency stop to cover the photographer with snow

technique known as the *emergency stop*, which you should also learn. It will enable you to avoid hitting unforeseen obstacles or colliding dangerously with other skiers.

● Approach in an upright position, with your arms slightly splayed.
● Drop the body suddenly, sharply turning the skis so that they become horizontal (i.e. at right angles to the fall line). At the same time edge the skis sharply while keeping the hips and upper body facing downhill.
● You will begin to skid, but you can shorten this phase by bending the upper body further forwards and pushing the knees more vigorously forwards and inwards.
● The more sharply you want to brake, the more heavily you should weight the outer ski.

We often use the emergency stop for fun in order to cover somebody with snow. But if you want to do that, you must first make sure that you have fully mastered the technique.

Bad visibility

If the visibility is poor, then skiing is no fun, and really good skiing is impossible. It is only by using your eyes that you are able to suit your technique to the terrain. If the visibility is poor, you soon get the feeling of having "unlearned" everything. Thus it can occasionally happen in races that top favourites lose while rank outsiders win outright, merely because of the fluctuating visibility.

● If the visibility is bad, you should try to get a feel for the terrain and snow conditions, and for any changes which may occur in them. The more tense you become, the less you will be able to use this sense. You should therefore stay as relaxed as possible, while remaining continually vigilant.
● Cut down your speed, so that you have time to react to any obstacles.
● Keep as close as you can to the *piste* markers.
● If possible, withdraw into more wooded terrain; the visibility is better.
● Never ski alone if you can help it; keep close to other skiers.
● Always confer with other skiers regarding visibility.

Bad luck with my equipment . . .

(as told by Christian)

"Neureuther in top form on the Jungfrau!" went the headline. And for once it was right. I was always at my best in the slalom on the "Jungfrau" *piste* at Wengen. And 1974 was no exception: I won with a completely new type of skis developed by Rossignol. These "secret weapons" were not even on the market yet; but I had managed to get hold of two sets of them: one for racing and one for training.

The racing skis were fantastic, so I used them as little as possible so as to preserve them. After the race, "Peter," I said to Endrass, my coach, "would you take my racing skis back to the hotel? I'll use the training skis for the prizegiving!"

I changed skis in the turmoil, and after the prizegiving I skied back to the hotel, scraping my skis on roots and stones where the snow was very thin. "Phew!" I said to myself, "aren't these skis running beautifully today! They're almost as good as the racing skis!"

When I had got back to my room, I held up the two damaged skis and stared at them in horror: "But they *are* my racing skis!" I nearly screamed with rage. And I never won a single race for the rest of that season . . .

Rosi once had a similar experience — but let her tell it to you in her own words. Rosi, what happened in Innsbruck that time?

"Well, it was like this: we were living in the Olympic village, but every day we travelled 25 miles to

Scharnitz for training, because the slalom slope there was very similar to the actual Olympic slope. Now it so happened that on the day before the Olympic slalom, I missed the team bus to Scharnitz. By then I had already won the gold in the downhill, but the discipline in the team was so strict at the time that no one took any notice of this fact. On the contrary, that evening I was required to pay a fine towards team funds . . .

"In the event a bobsleigh-driver gave me a lift to Scharnitz, which was really very kind of him. But I arrived at the slope only to get a good telling-off from the chief coach, Klaus Mayr: 'So you're going to do four extra runs — the others have done them already!'

"I was extremely annoyed by his tone of voice, because it wasn't really my fault that I had arrived late: the bus had simply stopped at a different place from where I had expected. My anger spurred me on, and I completed three quite

outstanding runs — at least, I thought they were outstanding — but Klaus Mayr could only say, 'Not bad — but try to ski a bit closer to the poles.'

"This made me angrier than ever. 'Rosi,' I said to myself, 'this time you're going to ski so close to the poles that you'll knock them all over! Don't leave a single one standing!'

"And this was exactly what I did: the poles toppled one by one — until I was the one to topple. I ran straight into a pole, breaking the tip of one of my skis. This wouldn't have been so bad if I hadn't decided to use my best racing skis for this final training session, so that I could really get used to them. So I had gone and broken my favourite skis.

"But it turned out better than for Christian in Wengen, and I was able to make up for the disappointment. The next morning I set out with the same self-confidence on a brand new set of skis, and went on to win the gold in the Olympic slalom . . ."

The equipment

According to recent statistics, about 3,000 skiers are involved in accidents every year in West Germany alone. Many of these accidents would never have happened if those concerned had used the correct equipment and had prepared themselves sufficiently beforehand.

Skiing is a highly technical sport, and for this reason everyone, from the beginner upwards, must take the greatest care to ensure that his equipment is right. For only then can you expect to make progress.

Ski equipment has come a long way since the beginning of the sport. Manufacturers these days must conform to stringent standards and safety regulations. Skis, boots, bindings and clips must all be compatible, and these, together with sticks and goggles, must conform to high safety standards. So that the purchaser knows that these standards have been met, many manufacturers send their products to be checked by various impartial bodies such as the TÜV in Bavaria and the International Standards Association. If a particular product is found to conform to the safety regulations, the manufacturer is then allowed to mark it with the stamp of the examining body concerned.

You should therefore make sure that you only buy equipment which is marked with such a safety standard.

There is a great variety of skiing equipment available, and the market is changing all the time. We would therefore recommend you to seek professional advice, which is usually available from a reputable supplier.

If you are a beginner, you should wait until you have had a little experience before embarking on the purchase of expensive equipment. By then you should know whether you are really keen to go on learning. All the equipment for your first skiing lessons can be easily hired from a ski school or a sports supplier.

The skis

In the 19th century, skis were first made of solid wood, and later of laminations. Modern skis are manufactured from polyethylene, metal, fibreglass and wood components.

The skis are constructed to suit the individual skier's requirements (from the beginner to the racer), and their characteristics will vary accordingly in terms of length, weight, breadth, flexibility and torsional rigidity.

The right choice of skis depends not so much on the size of the skier as on his individual skiing ability. You must therefore grade yourself according to the groups indicated on page 28 (L, A or S). Almost half of all skiers belong to group "A", so a further division has been introduced. If you can only ski at a moderate speed, use skidding steering, and prefer short swings and

You can't see the wood for the skis!

91

moguled *pistes*, then you should use skis of the "A_1" variety. But if you can produce long, carved turns on a completely smooth slope, then you belong to group "A_2".

The length of the skis: use the chart below to choose the correct ski length for you, bearing in mind that the taller, heavier skier should add anything up to 10cm, while the shorter, lighter person should buy skis which are anything up to 10cm shorter.

Every year the manufacturers bring out something new, such as "Compact Skis", "Mid Skis" or "Soft Skis"; these do not affect the length of the ski you need. "S"-skis are often indicated by the symbols "SL" or "RS", which stand for "slalom" and "giant slalom" (in German, "*Riesenslalom*").

Slalom skis are narrower, particularly in the waist, and are usually stiffer. They are thus very much easier to turn and edge, and have a very good grip. They also permit, and indeed require, the precise steering which only a well-trained expert can be expected to possess. These skis are also good for mogul racers, who love to produce short, fast swings on steep terrain.

"RS"-skis are not only suited to the giant slalom, but can be used in a variety of other disciplines. They also perform well in deeper snow. They produce longer turns, and run smoothly through the snow, even at high speeds. They are therefore a better type of ski for those whose technique is not quite 100 per cent.

"I"-skis are for those so-called individualists who are going to make unusually heavy demands on them — freestylers, for example, or off-*piste* skiers. They are also good for downhillers, who may even want lengths of up to 225cm. It is a well-known fact that the racing skis which are generally available are not so very different from those used by World Cup skiers. Such skis owe their remarkable qualities to perfect preparation and technical refinement.

On buying a new set of skis, you should immediately wax the bases and check that there are no burrs on the edges.

You should also check whether the steel edges rub audibly against each other when the bases are put together. If they do, then the edges are protruding, and will be continually cutting into the snow. In such cases you should either have the edges seen to or else ask for another pair. Only then will your skiing become enjoyable.

Skis and bindings should be protected from salt and dirt if they are to be carried on a roof rack. There are special ski bags for this purpose. We prefer to wrap them in blankets and put them inside the car, which gives 100 per cent protection. This also prevents extra noise and drag from the wind, and ultimately saves on fuel consumption.

Before storing the skis away for the summer, first repair the edges; then clean and wax the bases, without removing the surplus wax. They are best stored in a dry room. When the winter season comes round again, all you need to do is to remove the surplus wax from the bases, and the fun can begin.

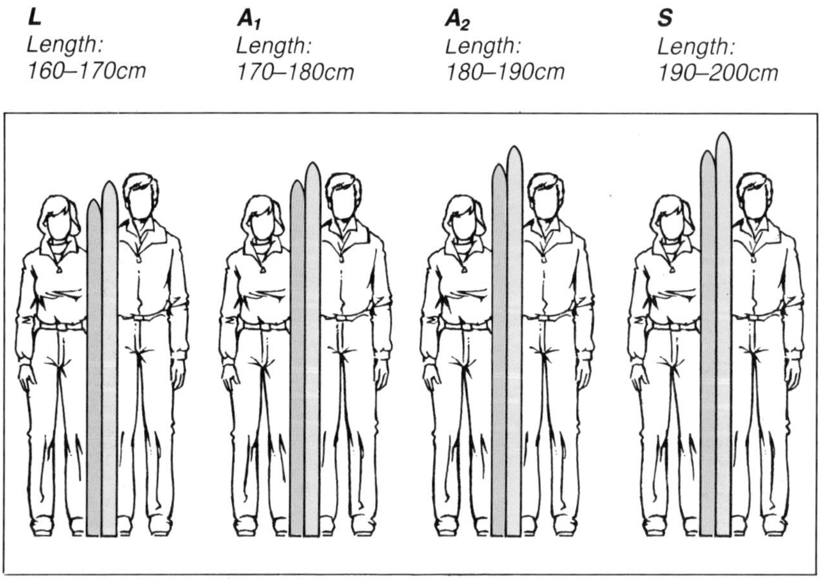

L	**A_1**	**A_2**	**S**
Length: 160–170cm	Length: 170–180cm	Length: 180–190cm	Length: 190–200cm

Skis are coded according to the type of skier who is intended to use them: 'L' for beginners, 'A_1' and 'A_2' for intermediates, and 'S' for experts

Care of the skis

As "top team" racers we were very fortunate: every morning we were presented with a pair of well-maintained, top-quality skis. Our equipment was kept up to scratch by qualified specialists, without whose assistance we could never have won any races.

Most skiers do not of course have the advantage of such personal service; so unless you are willing to have your skis repaired at a sports shop, you must do the job yourself. Every ski must be individually maintained and cared for, because its performance depends so much on the condition of the base and the edges. It has been proved experimentally that a new ski loses 60 per cent of its edge grip after only ten days' skiing. And after the same length of time its smoothness, and hence its ability to turn, has considerably deteriorated. However, it requires very little effort to restore the skis to the condition in which you bought them and to keep them in tip-top condition for many years.

But even a new ski needs a certain amount of work doing to it before it can be used. You should smooth off the edges, if necessary, with very fine emery paper, round off the tip and the tail, and wax and polish the base.

Ski maintenance does not require enormous skill, and you should have no trouble doing this at home, or even on holiday. There is a wide variety of different maintenance tools on the market, which make it as easy for the amateur as for the professional to manage fiddly jobs such as edge filing with considerable accuracy and success. However, the jobs described below are best carried out with the skis firmly clamped to a work bench.

Damage to the base

The first element of regular ski maintenance is attention to the base. Using a sharp steel scraper, remove any bumps or irregularities in the base, ensuring at the same time that it is fully flush with the edges. It should on no account be concave, and this you can also check with the scraper.

Small gouges should be filled in using a polyethylene candle. Polyethylene chips can also be used by melting them into the gouge with a soldering iron or a flat-iron. After that you should use a scraper on the base until it is completely smooth and even again.

Larger gouges cannot be filled in this way, as the polyethylene will tend to come out again as soon as you start skiing. The best method is to get hold of a piece out of an old ski base and glue it firmly into the gouge, having first carefully trimmed the gouge so the insert fits.

Care and sharpening of the edges

First check the edges for any obvious jagged areas, as these are usually too hard for the file to deal with. These jagged areas must be shaved off with a whetstone.

The actual filing process should be carried out using an edge file or a special sharpener. The latter is very much preferable, as it produces a guaranteed right-angled edge, and can also be otherwise adjusted as required. Start filing the underside edge first, until its whole surface gives an even surface sheen of "new metal".

You should at the same time file down the edges so that they are flush

with the base — on no account should the base be lower than the edges. The skis will then be easier to turn and less liable to catch in the snow.

Before you start to file the side of the edges, clamp the ski so that it is on its side. Again you should take great

care to produce a smooth, right-angled edge. File along the whole length of the ski except for the tip itself. To check if the edge is sharp enough, pass a finger-nail across it (not along it!). It should shave off just a curl of finger-nail. If you are a proper professional, you can then go on to produce a really clean finish using a fine file or emery paper.

After you have finished filing, dull off the edges by gently running a piece of fine emery paper (with a grit number of about 300) along their whole length. It

is always sensible to put a piece of emery paper in your pocket whenever you go skiing, so that you can quickly dull the edges if they "bite" too much. Beginners and intermediates tend to have to dull the edges rather more than experts. But in any case the inner edge should always remain sharper than the outer edge.

It is particularly important to dull the edges considerably more towards the ends of the skis (15–20cm back from the tips and 5–10cm forwards from the tails). You should do this with a piece of emery paper or a whetstone. This will stop the skis from "hooking" in the snow.

As soon as you have filed the edges, carefully remove all the stray metal shavings from the base. Then clean the base thoroughly with a cloth soaked in wax remover. Wait about half an hour, by which time the wax remover will have completely evaporated, before going on to wax the skis.

Waxing

Waxing skis is not difficult these days. The job can be done both quickly and without mess, using either a flat-iron or a special waxing iron. The choice of wax is no longer a problem either, because there is a wide variety of good quality waxes on the market. Basic paraffin wax is the best type for most skiers, though it should be mixed with other waxes for use in especially low temperatures. It is best to have the iron fairly hot, so that the wax can really penetrate the pores of the base. Then it will last much longer. Take an old flat-iron or a waxing iron, melt the wax against it and draw it in two long strands, first one way and then back along the base of the ski. Then run the iron along the whole length of the ski, spreading the wax evenly across the surface and pressing it into the pores.

After ironing, wait a few minutes for the wax to cool and harden; then use a plastic scraper to remove all excess wax so that wax is only left in the pores. Remove every bit of wax from the edges, and the ski is fully prepared for skiing.

You can of course also use tubes of wax or a cloth soaked in wax, but neither of these is as effective as waxing with a hot iron.

Wax for racing

Racing skis are waxed in much the same way as just described, but the wax itself must be carefully modified. The basic wax should be mixed with

other waxes for higher or lower temperatures. We also distinguished between harder and softer snow. If the snow is hard, icy or granular, we add some harder wax to the mixture. If the snow is soft, wet or sticky, we add a quantity of much softer wax, which tends to stop the snow from sucking on the skis.

No slalom or giant slalom has been won or lost on the basis of wax alone. It is the skill of the skier which is of primary importance in these disciplines. As for the skis themselves, it is only a question of whether or not they can grip on the icy surface.

Neither should the downhill racer have to depend on the wax on his skis — or at least not in theory. In modern downhill racing, the base of each individual pair of skis has been finely constructed to suit a particular temperature and type of snow. Franz Klammer, for example, has a choice of about 15 different pairs of skis for each race, and out of these he will choose the "winner" according to the snow and temperature conditions at the time. The skis are all carefully numbered, and the wax is mixed according to the particular conditions for which they are intended. In practice, however, it is often the choice of skis rather than the skiers' technique which determines who wins and who loses. Choosing the wrong set of skis can cost valuable seconds, which even the best racer cannot hope to win back.

The boots

Skiing is only a pleasure so long as your boots are comfortable, so choosing the right ski boots is extremely important. They must be chosen with great care, not according to their make, but by insisting on an exact fit for your own feet.

Note the following points:

● Decide which ability group you belong to (see page 28). The beginner in particular, and probably the intermediate too, should be quite happy with a boot which doesn't "lean" forward and is relatively soft in the shaft or cuff. A real expert's boots are characterised by a pronounced forwards lean, while the cuff is stiffer and usually longer.

It has been demonstrated that the average skier stands still on his skis for 20 times as long as he actually skis — a beginner for as much as 40 times as long. It is therefore sensible, if you buy boots which lean forwards, to make sure that they have an adjustment which will let you stand upright. Standing with your ankles flexed is uncomfortable and exhausting.

● Don't wear thick socks for trying boots on. Boots always stretch with time.

● Choose boots with orthopaedic insoles. These should also be removable, so that they can if necessary be replaced by insoles which have been specially tailored to your own feet.

● When you try boots on, check that the tongue fits comfortably and does not slip. You will otherwise be liable to get sore shins, as most of the power is transmitted via the area of the shins.

● If you can, go to a shop which is equipped with a special device for

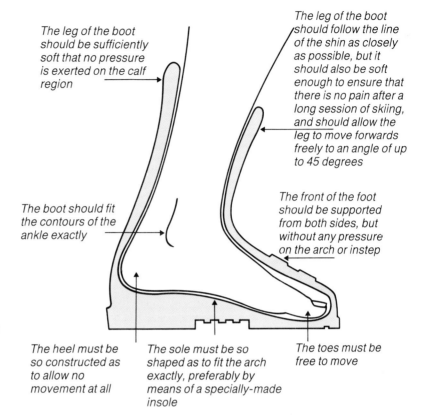

The leg of the boot should be sufficiently soft that no pressure is exerted on the calf region

The leg of the boot should follow the line of the shin as closely as possible, but it should also be soft enough to ensure that there is no pain after a long session of skiing, and should allow the leg to move forwards freely to an angle of up to 45 degrees

The boot should fit the contours of the ankle exactly

The front of the foot should be supported from both sides, but without any pressure on the arch or instep

The heel must be so constructed as to allow no movement at all

The sole must be so shaped as to fit the arch exactly, preferably by means of a specially-made insole

The toes must be free to move

simulating typical skiing movements. Otherwise you can never be completely sure that the boots can be used for skiing without causing discomfort or pain.

● Experts and racers will need especially well-fitting boots. Foam linings are very much to be recommended, as they help to compensate for irregularities in the feet.

● Boots have a tendency to change shape if they are not worn for a long time. If such is the case, don't wait until you are out on the slope before putting them on in the cold. Try them on the day before in the warmth of your room. You might

even warm them up with a hair-dryer first, which makes them very much easier to fit.

● If the boot pinches, take out the lining of the boot and cut or chisel bits out of the shell, or else out of the lining, at the points where it pinches. Be quite ruthless about this. Most good sports shops can also work wonders with a stretching machine to give you a good fit.

● If your foot feels sore, this is often caused by too much pressure on the instep. Take out the insole and either replace it with a thinner one or get rid of it completely. If necessary, cut a little bit out of the lining of the boot.

Playing tricks with the equipment

(as told by Christian)

After the 1976 Winter Olympics, Rosi had signed a contract with a firm of ski manufacturers. And as I was effectively engaged to her, it was felt that I really ought to use the same make.

The new skis were certainly marvellous for the ordinary skier, and great fun to use — but they simply didn't have enough grip to cope as well I would have liked with the icy slopes of the World Cup slalom. Indeed, at that time, in the winter of 1976/77, there were nothing *but* icy slopes to deal with. The result was that I kept skidding off course. We usually arrived at a World Cup venue some time in the evening, so it was often dark before I could walk down the course to see if it was iced up. If it glinted at me, then I knew I was going to have problems next day.

Wondering what to do next, I telephoned Wolfgang Junginger. Wolfgang was from Aschau, and had come third overall in the 1974 World Cup in St Moritz; but he had since given up top level racing, and was later to die tragically in an aeroplane accident in 1982. I asked him whether he might lend me a pair of his old racing skis, which were of a kind I had once used myself. The problem was that of finding a pair which didn't have the make written on the base. But my old friend "Juwo" was a real brick, and he found a pair for me . . .

I scraped off the upper surface of the skis and tried to paint them to look exactly like the new make of skis I was using. But the colour kept fading, and the next race loomed nearer and nearer. I rushed round all the silk-screen printers and paint shops I knew, but nobody could give me the right colouring.

We went off to Flims for our next race. And I spent the night before the slalom alone in the cellar, working away at these skis and terrified of being caught red-handed. But somehow I managed to make the colour stay at least until the morning. I had let my coach into the secret, so next morning he buried my skis in the snow so that no one would notice any difference. But then one of the servicing staff from the Erbacher firm took hold of one of my skis, pressed it hard in the middle and grinned at me rather spitefully: "Phew! Soft, aren't they! Now I know why you're always last, with your old foam-padded skis!" I grinned back even more spitefully — and came sixth in the race . . .

But one good thing came of all this: I gave up do-it-yourself painting, much to Rosi's delight, and without in the least feeling bad about it.

The next winter — that of 1977/78 — I tried the same trick, but this time with the giant-slalom skis which had won Rosi her silver in Innsbruck. They were specially made for skiing on ice. I also fitted them with a special design. But the holes in the mountings were too large — and I flew off my skis at the third gate, together with the bindings. I later had some sets of foreign skis "masked" professionally — but by then everybody in the skiing world knew all about my little tricks . . .

It was just the same story with my ski boots. Having the correct boots is essential for racing. It is not for nothing that Ingemar Stenmark has used exactly the same type of boot since 1975. He has stuck to it through thick and thin, in spite of a number of tempting offers from other manufacturers.

However, our DSV (German Skiing Federation) ski pool — the group of companies who supply equipment to the team — had no understanding of such niceties. Michael Veith and I had both used Dolomite boots for many years when they were suddenly banned. I could never get used to my new boots, so I decided to "convert" a pair of Dolomites to look like the ones I was supposed to wear. But by the end of the season somebody had guessed what I was up to and had "sneaked" on me. There was a terrific hullabaloo after this, and they refused to compensate me for "loss of earnings" — a privilege usually granted to those who had won or had done well in competitions. What most annoyed me was that Michael Veith had done exactly the same with his boots, but had managed to get away with it. What is more, "Fako" hadn't done half such a good job with them as I had. And as if that wasn't enough, he was being held up to me as a shining example of honesty!

Rosi had similar problems with her equipment in the 1968 Winter Olympics in Grenoble. There was a ruling at the time that all German skiers should use exclusively German products. So Rosi had decided to use Sohler skis for the downhill and Fritzmeiers for the giant slalom. The trouble was that

Fritzmeiers did not have exactly the right length of ski for Rosi, so her coach Sepp Behr thought she should use the Rossignol skis which she had used previously. But there was too little time left to "convert" the skis properly. So Sepp immediately covered the upper surface of the skis with a thick layer of silver racing wax, so as to obscure the Rossignol trade mark completely.

In those days the bases of skis were never marked by the firm, so that all skis looked exactly the same underneath. In her first run Rosi had achieved the sixth-best time, and she was just about to start her second run when a Frenchman appeared suddenly out of the blue. He beamed at her and wished her well. Then off she went. But during

the race she accidentally weighted the inside ski and fell. When she reached the finish she looked at the tips of her skis — and found something sticking to them. It was the Rossignol trade mark! The Frenchman had stuck it to her skis at the very last moment to get free publicity for his firm, and had unwittingly exposed the truth . . .

When I look back on it all now, I realise that this was only the very beginning of the "battle of the skis". The competition got tougher, and not many years later the only way to win the downhill was by wearing exactly the right skis at exactly the right time. It was also well known that the downhillers in the German team were not always provided with the fastest skis by foreign firms. So two of our DSV coaches — who shall

remain nameless — went on a secret mission during the Lauberhorn races at Wengen. They armed themselves with walkie-talkies and sneaked into the ski store belonging to an Austrian firm called Fischer — a real cloak-and-dagger operation ! They then "captured" two pairs of skis of a type which had proved particularly successful during the competition. These were the skis — and I make no bones about this — on which Michael Veith and Sepp Ferstl achieved their greatest triumphs in the downhill. Michael Veith used them to win the silver in the 1978 World Cup at Garmisch-Partenkirchen, in which Sepp Ferstl came fourth. Sepp later won twice on the very same skis, on the famous downhill course at Hahnenkamm . . .

The bindings

However good or expensive the bindings are, they are never any use unless they are properly adjusted. Every skier is of course fully aware of this; and yet examination of the bindings after ski accidents has frequently revealed the stupid risks which people take.

You should therefore note the following points:

● The determining factor when adjusting the bindings is the diameter of the leg at the top of the shin bone, which is measured with a special caliper square. The different settings for the bindings can all be read off at the same time, including those for women, men and children. The readings are of course only averages. Faster skiers should therefore adjust the figure up slightly, while smoother, gentler skiers should adjust the figure down.
● Have your bindings regularly tested by an expert, and especially before the beginning of the new season.
● All manufacturers these days mark their bindings according to the internationally-agreed IAS code, which is 1 to 3 for children, 3 to 6 for women and teenagers, and 4 to 10 for men. The figure which you have ascertained from the caliper square should be the same as the one in the middle of the adjustable scale which is given on your bindings. The bindings will work best for you if adjusted to this point on the scale.
● Make sure that the fittings and mountings are dealt with only by an expert.
● Use only those ski brakes which are appropriate to your particular bindings system. Special straps for locating buried skis (see page 81) are only useful for off-*piste* skiing.

● Never use toe and heel units of different makes.
● Only buy bindings which carry the safety certification mark.
● Always protect your bindings from salt and dirt by putting them in a ski bag. Otherwise they are liable to deteriorate badly.

Testing the release
The bindings should be adjusted by an expert, but you should also test them regularly yourself.

Testing by twisting: Place the ski so that it is tilted and edged in the snow. Try to release your boot from the bindings by twisting your leg. If this does not work, then the bindings should be readjusted or replaced.

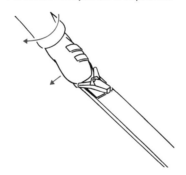

Testing by impact: Place the ski flat on the ground. Try to release the boot from the bindings by kicking it with the other foot. If you kick too lightly, the boot should then spring back to its original position.

The sticks

The ski stick is the least complicated item of the skier's equipment. But because of its shape it can easily be turned into a dangerous weapon. You should make sure that it conforms to safety standards and carries the appropriate certification mark.

The grip must be so shaped that it lies comfortably in the hand. It is important that the head of the grip should be sufficiently large to protect the hand. The buckle on the strap should be adjusted to allow the hand to move freely when the stick is hanging loose.

There are a number of sticks without straps on the market. They are equipped with a special integrated handle which is supposed to prevent the frequent thumb injuries to which skiers are prone. In use, however, these sticks are sometimes impractical, as they have to be continually held in the hand. Always try out ski sticks with ski gloves on!

The tip of the stick should be able to grip well in the ice, but should not be liable to cause injury. Hollow tips are probably the best for this. The length of your sticks should be exactly seven-tenths of your body height. If you find it difficult to work that out, try out the following tests:

● If you are still in the shop, turn the stick upside down and hold it immediately below the basket while resting it vertically on the ground. Your forearm should then be horizontal.
● If you are out on the snow, push the stick vertically into the snow as far as the basket. Your forearm should again be horizontal.

Peter Lüscher of Switzerland stages a spectacular fall in St Anton

Physical training

Fitness training for recreational skiers

Fitness is an everyday term, but it takes on a special significance in the area of sport. Here it is more than just a vague term implying good health: it describes the ability to achieve a specific, measurable, level of performance. A top sportsman can, for example, be said to be 100 per cent fit when he is capable of achieving 100 per cent performance in his particular sport. Fitness thus signifies the ability of the human body to withstand the physical stresses which the particular sport imposes. Each individual sport makes specific demands on the body, for which specific physical qualities are necessary. In basketball or volleyball, for example, taller people are physically better equipped than shorter people. Fitness, however, requires more than just physical qualities: it involves the whole person, in body, mind and spirit. Many sports — motor racing and mountaineering, for example — require a considerable element of courage. Psychological endurance, and the ability to submit to a regular and disciplined training schedule, are also vital elements of general sporting fitness. Fitness in sport thus implies not only a high level of performance, but also health, enjoyment and motivation.

Returning to the first aspect of fitness — that of performance and achievement — this is undoubtedly less vital to the recreational skier than to the committed racer; though it is true that a better performance means greater enjoyment, even if performance is not the main goal. What is meant, then, by physical fitness for the keen recreational skier? You need to be healthy in order to be physically fit; but, conversely, keeping fit also makes you much healthier. There is a lot you can do to be healthy: you can eat and sleep sensibly, drink alcohol only in moderation, and keep off smoking. But physical fitness has to be worked at: the body must be stretched in order to function more effectively. Your muscles and organs will only improve their performance if they are regularly exposed to physical stresses. These physical stresses can be so planned and organised that they bring about a steady improvement in the body's physical condition, and this is what fitness training is all about. Physical fitness for the keen recreational skier can be considered under three main headings:

● General endurance: this enables the body to cope effectively with physical stresses over a long period of time, without coming to any harm.
● Good strength training, so that the muscles not only become more powerful, but at the same time both support and protect the bone structure.

Gymnastics is an important part of the physical preparation for the winter season

- General mobility training: by this is meant not only the suppleness of the joints, but also the elasticity of the muscles.

You should train yourself successively in all three areas of physical fitness, according to your own physical needs and requirements. If you follow a sensible course of training, this will mean good health, general all-round fitness and a high level of performance in your skiing.

Endurance training

Endurance training forms the cornerstone of every good training programme. A specific course of endurance training puts extra physical demands on the body, to which it adapts by working more efficiently. The respiratory system benefits in particular. It functions more evenly and economically, and supplies the body more effectively with blood. The blood pressure also becomes better regulated. This improvement in the respiratory system is matched by similar adaptations in the musculature to meet the increased demands. Each group of muscles is trained to sustain effort more effectively.

The physical stresses involved in endurance training should be imposed evenly and gradually, and exercises should be interspersed with short rests. It is this which enables the body to adapt in the appropriate way. Increase the physical demands only gradually, and carefully control their intensity according to your pulse rate. The following formulae will be of assistance here:

- Minimum pulse rate = 180 minus your age
- Maximum pulse rate = 210 minus your age

If you are 40, for example, your pulse rate during endurance training should lie between 140 (=180 − 40) and 170 (=210 − 40). Your general endurance training is therefore quite sufficient if you train so as to achieve the minimum pulse rate, which is 140 in this particular example.

The following activities are appropriate to a course of general endurance training (the times and the distances given are those appropriate to a man aged between 35 and 40):

- Swimming for about 20 to 40 minutes, over a distance of 1000 to 1500 metres. You may choose whichever style you prefer, though back stroke is particularly good for that long-suffering spine.
- Cycling for about 60 to 90 minutes, choosing a route which is as flat as possible. If you are using a racing bike, you should cover a distance of between 25 and 40 kilometres (16–25 miles), though you should avoid using too high a gear.
- Jogging for about 20 to 40 minutes, over a distance of between 4 and 8 kilometres (2½–5 miles), on a relatively flat route. Make sure that you wear a good pair of running shoes, so that your feet, ankles and knees do not suffer unnecessarily.

Any form of training should work and stretch the muscles and develop the heart, but it should never make unreasonable demands on the tendons, ligaments and joints. You should therefore choose forms of endurance training which strain the joints as little as possible. From this point of view, swimming and cycling are far easier on the joints than jogging. It is best to vary the form of exercise according to the weather and season, and to your own personal inclinations. In winter, cross-country skiing can also be used as a form of endurance training.

Strength training

Do not be worried by this term. Strength training can be extremely varied, and does not simply mean lifting heavy dumb-bells and working with weight-training machines.

For recreational skiers body weight alone is all that is needed to provide appropriate forms of strength training. Strength training is intended

to improve the work of the muscles. Each individual muscle learns to produce more energy, while the muscles together become better co-ordinated. There are two main types of strength training:

- dynamic or isotonic training, in which the body is trained to move specific weights;
- static or isometric training, in which the body is trained to work against a specific resistance without moving.

Isometric training is not very well suited to our purposes, and has a number of disadvantages. Dynamic training involves the choice of about three to six different exercises, each of which is geared to a particular group of muscles. You should repeat each exercise a specific number of times, depending on the physical demands it imposes and on your own individual performance level. Each exercise is followed by a rest of between two and three minutes. This particular training method is probably already familiar to you under the name *circuit training*. A circuit of about four different exercises is usually quite sufficient for an amateur sportsman. No weights are used apart from that of the body itself, so it should not be a difficult training programme to organise.

2nd Exercise: for training the stomach muscles:
Lie stretched out on your back; then lift both legs simultaneously, while at the same time raising the upper body so that the hands can be clapped together behind the legs. Repeat this 10 to 15 times, then rest for two minutes.

3rd Exercise: for training the arm and shoulder muscles:
A push-up, leading to a kneel.
Repeat this 15 to 20 times, then rest for two minutes.

1st Exercise: for training the leg muscles:
Alternate between a half knees-bend and standing on tiptoe. Repeat this 20 to 30 times, then rest for two minutes.

4th Exercise: for training the back and seat muscles:
Lie stretched out on your stomach with your arms out in front; simultaneously raise your arms, chest and legs. Repeat this 10 to 15 times, then rest for two minutes.

You should work through these exercises two or three times a day according to the instructions given above. Do not forget to keep your breathing regular throughout, whatever the effort involved. Use the rests between exercises to relax the muscles you have been using.

Mobility training

As we have already explained, mobility training should be aimed, not only towards improving the suppleness of the joints, but also towards stretching the muscles and making them more elastic. Modern gymnastics are undoubtedly the most effective way of achieving this, though gymnastic exercises can vary enormously depending on the type of sport for which they are intended. Stretching exercises are also a very effective form of mobility training.

Building up a training programme

Now that we have covered the three most important forms of fitness training — endurance, strength and mobility — it remains to consider how they should be organised into an effective fitness programme. You should plan beween three and four training sessions per week, and allocate these sessions as follows:

1st day: endurance training
2nd day: strength training
3rd day: endurance training (perhaps in a different form from that used on the 1st day)
4th day: mobility training

If you want to be completely fit, then regular training is the only answer. And it is no good letting it drop whenever you don't feel up to it, as this will only mean starting all over again. Your fitness programme should become a regular feature of your timetable for the week. Before long you will be feeling a lot healthier, and your sporting performance will improve correspondingly. As your fitness improves, so the work load will begin to feel less demanding, and you might well consider running for longer, repeating the exercise more frequently, or even having an extra training session each week.

Conditioning for the serious competitor

In order to succeed, the international sportsman must strive to reach peak condition. By this we mean the highest possible level of physical fitness. However, such peak condition can only be maintained for a limited period of time, beyond which no amount of further training can be expected to sustain it. Thus an international sportsman's physical condition must follow a continuous cycle of peaks and troughs. The aim of conditioning is to ensure that this cycle is correctly timed, so that the sportsman will reach his physical peak at the same time as an important event or competition. This is what is known as "peaking". A skier must of necessity reach his peak during the course of the winter. The timing of this peak depends on a number of interdependent factors, which can be defined under the following headings.

General endurance (stamina): The ability of the body to sustain a certain level of performance over a relatively long period of time.

General muscular strength: The ability of the body's muscles to produce a certain level of power in relation to the weight of the body.

Mobility: The suppleness of all the joints, combined with the elasticity of all the muscles.

Speed: The ability of the body to work with maximum speed and agility within a short period of time (reaction time is also included in this category). Sprinting is a good example of this.

Muscular power (anaerobic): A specific type of muscular power, whereby the muscles achieve their maximum power output within a short period of time.

Muscular endurance (aerobic): Endurance with reference to specific groups of muscles, whereby they achieve their maximum power output over a longer period of time. This is, for example, particularly important for rowing.

Speed endurance: A specific form of endurance, describing the ability of the body to achieve maximum speed and agility over a certain period of time. Middle-distance running is a good example of this.

These different aspects of conditioning are further categorised under two headings:

General conditioning: Those aspects of conditioning which are vital to the body's general performance, and upon which later, more specialised conditioning is based. There is only an indirect connection between general conditioning and the

sport for which conditioning is required.

Specific conditioning: Those aspects of conditioning which, although built upon a course of general conditioning, are specifically aimed at a particular sport.

A course of condition training for Alpine skiing can be subdivided as follows:

General conditioning:
● General endurance
● Strength
● Speed
● Mobility

Specific conditioning:
● Anaerobic power
● Muscular endurance (for downhill and giant slalom)
● Speed endurance (for slalom)

Such a programme may be organised entirely differently in the case of other disciplines. In cross-country skiing, for example, aerobic endurance is as much a part of specific as of general conditioning. The exercises which make up the specific conditioning programme should be exactly geared to the kinds of demands which skiing imposes.

Planning a training programme

If you want to peak at a particular time, then it is vital to plan your training programme according to an exact timetable. Thus training is no longer a random series of exercises, but a carefully planned programme, specifically aimed at producing the highest possible peak of performance at a particular time. There are two main factors here:

● The amount of training: the length of the individual training exercises, and their frequency over the period concerned

- The intensity of training: the degree of overload in comparision with the level of performance so far

The organisation of an effective conditioning programme requires an accurate assessment of the amount and intensity of the training involved, which should include exactly the right combinations of exercises, both of a general and of a specific nature.

The training year can be divided into three main parts:

- The preparation period: The part of the year during which the skier builds up his physical condition so as to peak during the competition period.
- The competition period: The part of the year during which all the skiing competitions take place — in particular the high points of the different competitions.
- The transition period: The part of the year following the competition period, during which the skier's performance deteriorates, but which provides him with an opportunity to rest before the beginning of the next preparation period.

These three training periods are further subdivided into smaller units, which ultimately divide into the individual training sessions.

The training programme must be organised according to the specific needs of the individual. It is indeed only by tailoring the programme to his own individual strengths and weaknesses that a sportsman's condition can be expected to benefit. We shall, however, make a few general points concerning the planning of a training programme, using the example shown in the diagram below. Most learning methods start with the general and move on to the specific, and this is equally true of condition training. You should start with a programme of fairly general exercises, and wait until the end before moving on to exercises more specific to the competition. The decisive factor, as we have already pointed out, is careful planning of the amount and intensity of training, both of which should be gradually increased during the course of the prepartion period. Then, as the competition period begins, the amount of training should decrease considerably, while the intensity of training should be further increased so as to reach a peak. Condition training and skiing training should never be

A physical training schedule

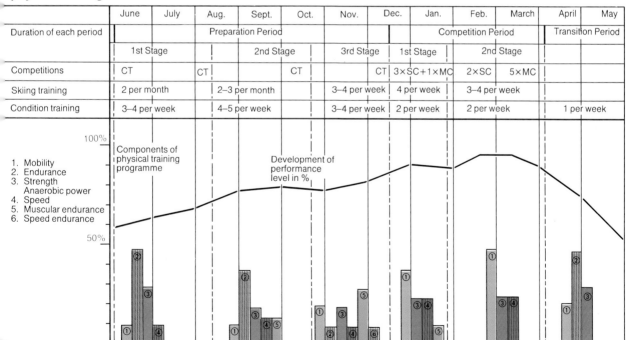

	June	July	Aug.	Sept.	Oct.	Nov.	Dec.	Jan.	Feb.	March	April	May
Duration of each period			Preparation Period					Competition Period			Transition Period	
	1st Stage			2nd Stage		3rd Stage		1st Stage		2nd Stage		
Competitions	CT		CT		CT		CT	3×SC+1×MC	2×SC	5×MC		
Skiing training	2 per month		2–3 per month			3–4 per week	4 per week	3–4 per week				
Condition training	3–4 per week		4–5 per week			3–4 per week	2 per week	2 per week		1 per week		

1. Mobility
2. Endurance
3. Strength
   Anaerobic power
4. Speed
5. Muscular endurance
6. Speed endurance

Components of physical training programme

Development of performance level in %

Key to abbreviations
▶ CT = Condition test
▶ SC = Secondary competitions
▶ MC = Main competitions

105

considered separately, though it may of course be useful to keep a distinction for planning purposes. The condition training programme on the previous page should therefore be considered in conjunction with the skiing training programme on page 128. The particular example we have chosen is for a skier who has not yet reached the national squad, but who fully intends to win regional championships. He is assumed to be aged between 15 and 24, and of full training capacity, though with little or no opportunity for skiing during the summer and early autumn. Skiing training is thus mostly confined to the winter season. But any skier of such calibre will have a lot going for him if he can combine hard training with the necessary flair and application.

General endurance training

The advice we would give for general endurance training for the professional is much the same as that for fitness training for the amateur (see page 101). The previous training you have done will mean you can considerably increase the amount of training you do now, though the intensity of training should remain relatively low. Skiers up to the age of 30 should aim for a pulse rate between 140 and 160 per minute, while those who are well above that age should follow the rules given on page 102.

The three most important forms of general training are swimming, cycling and jogging, though cross-country skiing can provide a good alternative during the winter. At first you should train according to the *continuous* method. This means that the pulse rate remains reasonably constant, between 140 and 160, throughout the training session. Once you have got into a routine, you may decide to change to *interval training*. This means that the intensity is increased for a

short period, and then correspondingly decreased for a similarly short period. This alternation of high- and low-intensity exercise should cause the pulse rate to fluctuate between 180 and 130, but you should never actually rest during the training session itself. Interval training may well come naturally as a result of going up and down hills while jogging or cycling. The training sessions should run approximately as follows, depending on the type of training chosen:

- Swimming: 30–40 mintues; 1500–2000 metres.

- Cycling: 90–120 minutes; 40–70 kilometres.

- Jogging: 40–60 minutes; 8–12 kilometres.

These days there are a number of instruments on the market for measuring the pulse rate during training sessions. They can be adjusted for individual types of training.

Strength

This term covers much the same area of training as was considered in the basic introduction on page 102. But strength training for more advanced skiers necessarily involves a far more thorough consideration of every muscle in the body. Too much concentration on the leg muscles at the expense of the rest will destroy the delicate balance of the body's muscle system, whereas general training of all the muscles together will lead to a marked improvement in your skiing technique. Here is an example of a simple but effective circuit-training programme, which makes provision, not only for the general training of the whole muscle system, but also for that

equally vital element known as anaerobic power (see page 104). A sandbag has been included as a means of increasing the intensity of the exercises, but they can if necessary be practised without this.

1st Exercise: Move from the straddle position into alternate one-legged half knee-bends, lifting the free leg up to the level of the knee which has been bent. Hold the sandbag across the small of the back so as to give support to the spine.
(40 times, lifting first the left leg, then the right, alternately)

2nd Exercise: Lie on your stomach with your feet held down by your partner or the wall-bars: lift your body and turn to the left; lie down again; lift your body and turn to the right . . . and so on. Hold the sandbag across the back of your neck. (15 times)

rd Exercise: From an upright position, jump up into a squat position. No sandbag needed. (15 times)

th Exercise: Hold the sandbag at each end with your palms upwards: lift over the top of your head to the back of your neck, and then return it to the original position. 5 times)

th Exercise: Lie on your back with your feet held down: sit up and turn to the left; lie down again; sit up and turn to the right . . . and so on. Hold the sandbag across the back of your neck. 5 times)

You should rest for two minutes between each exercise, so as to enable you to recover before the next one. You should carry out this series of exercises either twice or three times, depending on what stage you have reached in your programme. Relax your muscles completely during the rests, so that you can give full power to the next exercise.

Speed

We have not dealt with speed training at all so far, as it is not considered necessary for amateur skiers. The type of training involved also depends rather more on the particular sport or discipline concerned. Speed is defined as the ability of the body to achieve the maximum speed and agility within a short period of time. This also includes that all-important factor known as reaction time. Speed depends to a large extent on muscular power — in particular anaerobic power. Speed training should therefore be built up on the basis of an initial strength-training programme. The exercise should be short in duration but of high intensity. You should also have plenty of rest in between exercises, so that the body can make an almost complete recovery each time. Here are some examples of possible exercises:

● Commando-style sprints over a distance of 30 metres, using a variety of starting positions, such as lying on the back or stomach, or sitting cross-legged. (8–12 times, with rests of 2–3 minutes)
● "To-and-fro" sprints over a distance of 50 metres: steadily increase the running speed to a maximum, hold this speed for a few seconds, and relax the effort so as to slow down naturally to a halt. (8–12 times, with rests of 2–3 minutes)

Make sure that the muscles are thoroughly warmed up before doing

any of these exercises. Otherwise you will run the risk of straining or tearing a muscle.

Specific endurance training

(Muscular endurance and speed endurance)
Muscular endurance training requires an initial level of general training in both strength and endurance. The term refers to the ability of the muscles to produce a high level of power output over a considerable length of time. Muscular endurance is the chief performance factor in the downhill and giant slalom, while the slalom also depends for its success upon a sufficient level of muscular endurance. Circuit training is the best method to employ here. Each exercise is designed to place a very heavy load on a specific group of muscles, with only very short rests in between. This is because the development of good muscular endurance depends on working hard while in a state of

exhaustion. The sequence of exercises which follows is only one of many possible circuits which may be considered appropriate to the development of muscular endurance:

1st Exercise: Alternate one-legged angle jumps, lifting up the free foot to the level of the opposing knee.

2nd Exercise: Lie flat on your back with your arms outstretched: lift up your arms and legs simultaneously as high as they will go, if possible so that the hands and feet meet in the middle.

3rd Exercise: Start in running position, clapping your hands together above your head; jump into straddle position, clapping your hands on your hips; jump back to running position again . . . and so on.

4th Exercise: Lie on your stomach with your arms outstretched: raise your arms and legs simultaneously up and down, repeating this at a fast tempo.

5th Exercise: Start in an upright position with your hands stretched upwards; touch your toes; return to the original position; bend your knees;

keep repeating this sequence at a fast tempo.

6th Exercise: A type of squat thrust, alternating between front support position with legs apart and squat position.

Practise each exercise intensively for 20 seconds, gradually increasing the time up to 40 seconds as the training proceeds. The rests between each exercise should be correspondingly shortened from an initial time of 40 seconds to one of 20 seconds. Repeat the whole sequence twice or three times, with one- to two-minute rests between each sequence.

Speed endurance, like muscular endurance, plays a vital role in the skier's specific training programme. The training should be based on a thorough grounding in general endurance and speed training. Speed endurance refers to the body's ability to produce a high level of speed and agility over a longer period of time. Speed endurance is vital to slalom performance, and important though less vital to other disciplines. Courses in speed endurance training are structured on similar lines to those used for muscular endurance, in that the exercises are of a high intensity with only short rests in between. The training programme is mostly made up of running exercises. Here is an example of the form they might possibly take:

- 100-metre sprint (repeat 8–19 times)
- 200-metre sprint (repeat 6–8 times
- a series of sprints of increasing length:
  3×100m — 2×200m — 1 × 300m
- a series of runs of decreasing length:
  1×600m — 2×400m — 3×200m

Both forms of specific endurance training depend very much on the sport or discipline for which they are intended. You should plan a training session so that it can be followed by a long period of rest, during which you can make a complete recovery. In other words, you should never carry on immediately into another form of conditioning or skiing training.

Mobility

This area has already been considered in the section for amateurs (see page 103). Good mobility is absolutely essential for skiers, but alas, skiing does not necessarily make for mobility — which means that regular, all-year-round mobility training is a must for all skiers. Gymnastics is the most common type of mobility training. One of the most popular forms of gymnastics today is the form known as *aerobics*, in which a series of rhythmic exercises is practised against a musical background. This is good for developing endurance as well as mobility. Good gymnastics can come in a wide variety of forms, depending on the purpose for which it is intended.

Additional forms of training

Here are some suggestions as to how you might make your training programme more varied and interesting. There are, for example, a vast number of different sports which are not only enjoyable in themselves but can also assist the conditioning process. And the more variety you can build into your training programme, the more motivated you will be. The following sports may be of help in the development of certain aspects of fitness:

- Football (speed endurance, reaction time)
- Volleyball and basketball (jumping power, reaction time)
- Tennis (speed and reaction time)
- Rowing and canoeing (muscular endurance)
- Mountaineering (general endurance, muscular endurance)
- Hill-walking (general endurance)
- Windsurfing (muscular endurance, general dexterity)
- Trial and BMX (muscular endurance, general dexterity)

Leisure sports do not, however, provide the basis for a conditioning programme: they are merely added extras. The same applies to the list of activities below, which includes a number of suggestions as to healthful and relaxing ways of spending your rest periods:

- Good healthy living, with plenty of sleep and the right sort of food
- Sauna
- Massage
- Swimming in warm water
- Relaxation training
- Non-sporting activities, such as working, reading, philosophising, looking for mushrooms, and so on.

A good all-round performance in skiing depends on a healthy balance of training and leisure activities.

Fitness is vital if you are to perform well throughout the winter season

How fit am I? — a fitness test

This is a test to show how fit you are, or rather how much fitter you are becoming. It has been specially organised to test those aspects of fitness which are relevant to skiing. You should carry out a test of this sort at least once every two months, or preferably monthly. You can then test your level of improvement and adjust your training programme accordingly. The test consists of three exercises in which you jump over a pair of skis or a similar set of markings, using your ski sticks to support you.

You should repeat each exercise over a period of 30 seconds, trying to jump over your skis as many times as possible within that time. Rest for 60 seconds before going on to the next exercise. If you become exhausted before the half-minute is up, then you should stop earlier and add the time left over to the minute's rest. The test is measured according to the number of times you repeat each exercise. There are effectively two jumps to every repetition. In other words, you will have completed the exercise once when you have jumped back to the side of the skis from which you began. Either count the number of repeats yourself, or else ask your partner to count them for you. The result of the test will be the sum of all the repeats in all three exercises. You can then use the chart opposite to assess your own degree of fitness. Comparison with the results of previous tests will indicate how much your fitness has improved.

We wish you the best of luck with your training programme!

1 top: Jumping over the skis from one leg to the other, on each occasion lifting the free foot up to the level of the opposite knee.

2 middle: Jumping sideways over the skis with both legs together.

3 bottom: Jumping forwards and backwards over the skis with both legs together

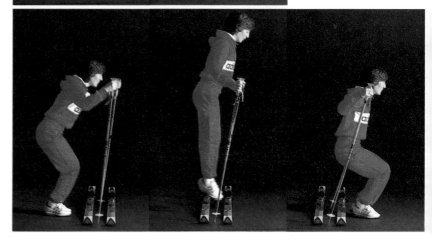

Test assessment

The assessment:

1 You are in peak condition for the winter season.
2 Your condition is satisfactory, but with further training you could be even fitter.
3 More regular training would certainly do no harm.
4 Much room for improvement.

How the assessement is reached:

The table is graded for professionals. Amateurs should add 20 points to their score before making their assessment.

	Score	Assessment
Men	over 150	1
	135–149	2
	120–134	3
	100–119	4
Women	over 130	1
	115–129	2
	95–114	3
	75– 94	4

Our scores:

The results of tests made on 15 July 1983:

Rosi: 132 points
Christian: 154 points

Even heavyweight skiers have their own special championship in the United States — though most who are overweight are best advised to do some fitness training

Tips for the racer

Alpine racing

Most skiers enjoy the sport of skiing for its own sake, but for some it is also a keenly competitive sport. Competitive skiing is a highly skilled activity, requiring courage, technical ability, peak fitness and the willingness to take risks. The more highly skilled the competition, the more it becomes a subject for general discussion and a spectator sport for skiers and non-skiers alike. Our many-faceted society gives sportsmen the chance to aim for the top, and, more than that, to reach new heights of skill and achievement. When records are broken, then every skier, whatever his level of ability, can dream of what even he could achieve, if only he were better or had the time.

Alpine racing has an incredible fascination for both spectators and skiers alike.

Every winter thousands of people flock to the classic events at great European centres such as Kitzbühel, Wengen and Garmisch-Partenkirchen. The skiers themselves are so infected by the spirit of competition that all their previous defeats, disappointments and injuries are completely forgotten in the face of new excitements and challenges.

Alpine racing is divided into three main disciplines: the slalom, the giant slalom and the downhill. In the

1982/83 season yet another competition was added: the so-called super-giant slalom, which lies somewhere between the downhill and the giant slalom. Some events are made up of more than one discipline, such as the classic Arlberg-Kandahar combination, which includes both downhill and slalom racing. Success in Alpine racing is measured on the basis of stopwatch timing, the aim being to complete a given course in the shortest possible time. The fastest skier is the winner. Alpine racers are pitted against one another, though only indirectly, since each competitor must complete the course alone. Alpine racing is thus in some ways a rather solitary sport, except to the extent that competitors belong to a team, with whom they train throughout the year. All through the winter season they must live and work together, and observe their progress as they compete against each other. For it is only by comparing his time with those of his rivals that a racer can get any idea of how well he is doing. Therefore the better the team, the more successful the individual competitor within it.

In this chapter we shall first give a brief description of each of the three classical disciplines, and then go on to consider a number of technical and tactical points which may be of assistance to skiers wishing to develop a good competition technique. But first one important

ngemar Stenmark: the perfect echnician

general point: performance in competitions depends primarily on technique. Not until you are technically fully in command can your performance be expected to benefit from other factors such as fitness and tactics. An Alpine racer should have achieved a good all-round technique between the ages of 10 and 15. His technique should also be fully in tune with other essential features, such as equipment, muscle power and general physical fitness. You will never make any further progress until you have fully mastered every aspect of technique.

Slalom

What is slalom?

The key to slalom racing is a perfect mastery of fast turning techniques. In theory the slalom requires no more than the usual skiing techniques. But modern slalom in practice is a far more highly-skilled affair. Indeed, the competitor must almost be an acrobat to win. A good slalom course should allow the skier to make a smooth descent through a variety of different gates and terrains. It should also be so designed as to require the maximum variation in the radius and frequency of turns. The slalom race is always run on two different courses, which are laid out to the following specifications:

● The height difference between the start and the finish:
130–180 metres for women in the Winter Olympics
180–220 metres for men in the Winter Olympics
120–180 metres for women in international competitions

140–200 metres for men in international competitions

● The number of gates:
For women, a minimum of 45 and a maximum of 60
For men, a minimum of 55 and a maximum of 75

The course must include five hairpin gates and two verticale or flush gates.
Slalom is to Alpine racing as sprinting is to flat racing. The hallmarks of the slalom skier are speed and quick reactions, together with really good techniques. Good race performance also requires

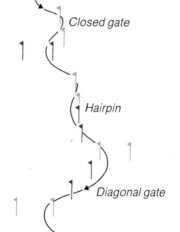

Open gate

Closed gate

Hairpin

Diagonal gate

"Verticale" or "Flush"

decisiveness and perfect concentration. The outcome of the race can be determined by differences of only a hundredth of a second. The modern slalom *piste* is usually hard and icy, which calls for technical precision and good equipment.
Since the 1982 World Championships at Schladming, flexible self-redressing slalom poles have been used in most of the big competitions, which means the racer can risk skiing much closer to these poles. The result of this is that the slalom has become even more dynamic, competitive and exciting than previously.

Technique in slalom

The slalom presents a great variety of different situations, and so entails considerable technical versatility. A technique which is too one-sided will drastically limit the skier's performance. It is, however, possible to talk of a basic slalom swing, which is then modified and varied according to the circumstances. Slalom skiing requires accurate steering on a hard course, for which two things are absolutely essential:

● one-legged skiing

● pronounced and effective vertical movement

By one-legged skiing is meant extreme weighting of the outer ski in the swing, together with effective weight transfer on swing release. The basic form of weight transfer used in the slalom is the step turn with open parallel stemming (see page 53). The stemming can then be modified to an ordinary uphill stem or an uphill scissor, depending on the circumstances. Good vertical movement will increase edge grip and enhance the fine control of the edging. The end of the swing should be characterised by the sudden

terruption of a downwards
movement leading straight into an
upwards movement. This ensures the
maximum possible edge grip at the
end of the swing. The vertical
movement in the slalom should follow
the same pattern as the basic parallel
swing, though the timing of the vertical
movement, so vital to slalom
technique, is subtly different:

● The body does not move
downwards until the end of the
swing.

● The sudden interruption of the
downwards movement should lead
immediately into the upwards
movement.

Careful timing of vertical movement at
the end of the swing enables the skis
to turn both quickly and accurately into
the next swing. The edges grip
hardest at the end of the swing; but
the skis then become completely
unweighted, even to the extent of
rising off the ground — which means
they can be turned quickly into the

*A study in comparative technique:
Andreas Wenzel, Bruno Nöckler and
Peter Lüscher*

new swing. But it is not because of this
unweighting that vertical movement is
so vital to the slalom, but because of
the extreme weighting and edge grip
which is needed at the end of the
swing. The inner stick must be placed
firmly, particularly if the slope is steep
or the turn is a sharp one. It should
also be planted well to the side so as
to provide maximum support, thus

considerably assisting the turning of the skis. Given that your course usually runs very close to the slalom poles, it is important to bring the hand close to the body as soon as the stick has been planted, so that the arm and shoulder can slip easily past the pole.

To sum up then: basic slalom technique requires extreme weighting of the outer ski, effective weight transfer and vertical movement, maximum edge grip at the end of the swing and effective use of the stick.

Two variants of slalom technique have already been mentioned, using weight transfer by means of uphill stemming and uphill scissor. Jet movement (see page 67) can also be incorporated as a means of acceleration. This requires good stick technique to support the body as the legs are thrust forward. Jet movement usually begins after the lowering of the body at the end of the swing, and the body is not raised again until the skis are turned into the new swing. At points where the course turns very sharply, an element of anticipation is also required. This leads to a flexing of the muscles which makes the skis easier to turn. If there are a lot of ruts in the course — which often happens when the *piste* becomes soft for a while — then good compensation technique is also very useful.

Slalom skiing can display a wide variety of different forms and combinations of techniques, depending on the circumstances and on the individual skier. But competition performance depends very much on how well the skier is able to combine these techniques so as to match the requirements of the course.

Tactics in slalom

By tactics is meant the way in which the skier uses the different techniques available to the greatest possible advantage, so as to produce the best possible result. Versatility is vital to good slalom tactics, but it is not everything. Equally important is the ability to match the technique to the circumstances. The basic technique should be modified in the following ways depending on the nature of the particular part of the course:

- Steep terrain:
  ○ extreme weighting of the outer ski
  ○ firm stick planting
  ○ step turns with uphill stemming

- Shallow terrain:
  ○ step turns with uphill scissor

- Hard, icy *piste*:
  ○ extremely pronounced vertical movement

- Soft, often rutted *piste*:
  ○ step turns with uphill stemming
  ○ compensation technique

- Sections with sharp turns
  ○ step turns with uphill stemming
  ○ anticipation
  ○ jet movement

- Smooth sections, with very shallow corners
  ○ step turns with uphill scissor
  ○ no stick planting, even during the swing

Tactics are especially important at the points where the terrain changes, or where the radius and rhythm of the swing must be altered. It is vital to change the technique and the course of the swing at exactly the right moment. It is generally true that there is more time to be gained from sharp swings than from shallow swings, but there is also more time to be lost!

Bojan Križaj

Giant slalom

What is giant slalom?

The giant slalom course should provide for a good variety of swings of different sizes. The route to be taken between the gates is very much left to the individual. The giant slalom never has a series of gates along the fall line like the vertical sections of the slalom. The best courses are those which make full use of the breadth of the slope. The specifications of the giant slalom are as follows.

● The height difference between the start and the finish:

   250–350 metres for women
   250–400 metres for men
   (In World Cup races the lower limit is set at 300 metres for both women and men)

● The number of gates:
   15 per cent of the height difference (in metres) of the actual course, allowing for a variation of up to plus or minus five

The giant slalom, like the slalom, is held on two different courses. With an execution time of between one minute twenty and one minute forty per run, it demands a high level of muscular endurance, especially in the leg muscles. The skis are between five and ten centimetres longer than slalom skis. Alpine racers should wear special aerodynamically-designed clothing for the sake of speed. Wearing a special racing suit instead of the usual ski trousers and jumper can mean a saving of as much as one second per minute in the giant slalom. Many experts consider the giant slalom to be the most difficult of the Alpine disciplines. Success in the giant slalom depends on so many different factors: perfect technical skill,

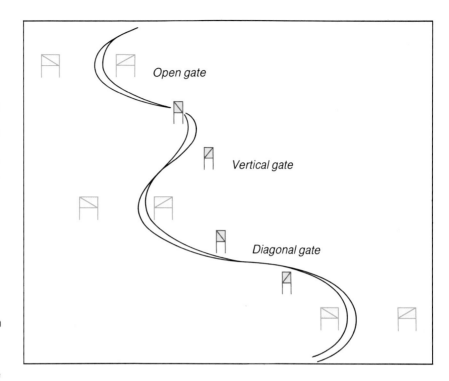
Open gate
Vertical gate
Diagonal gate

coupled with peak fitness, and an ability to determine the optimum speed and the route which skis should take between the gates. But in spite of the heavy demand which it makes, the giant slalom is not so popular with spectators, as even the most perfect run can be visually somewhat unspectacular.

Technique in giant slalom

A skier's technique in the giant slalom should be geared towards accelerating as much as possible and braking no more than absolutely necessary. Performance will be greatly enhanced by modfying the basic techniques in the following ways:

● smooth, rounded swings

● accurate aiming and steering of the skis so as to keep the track as narrow as possible

● step turns with uphill scissor to produce acceleration

● minimal friction when sliding

● giving full consideration to aerodynamics, especially at high speeds.

These considerations lead us to a number of basic principles which apply to the giant slalom. There is a form of swing which is basic to the giant slalom, though as with the slalom it admits of a number of variations. The skis must be turned very gradually during the swing so as to produce a smooth, rounded track. At the initiation of the swing, turn the skis gently, taking full account of the speed and radius of the swing. Most skiers instinctively turn them too sharply at first, causing the skis to skid sideways during the swing. The outer ski must

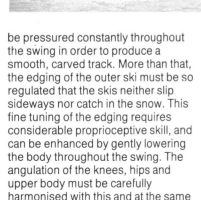
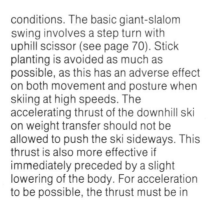

be pressured constantly throughout the swing in order to produce a smooth, carved track. More than that, the edging of the outer ski must be so regulated that the skis neither slip sideways nor catch in the snow. This fine tuning of the edging requires considerable proprioceptive skill, and can be enhanced by gently lowering the body throughout the swing. The angulation of the knees, hips and upper body must be carefully harmonised with this and at the same time adjusted to the external

conditions. The basic giant-slalom swing involves a step turn with uphill scissor (see page 70). Stick planting is avoided as much as possible, as this has an adverse effect on both movement and posture when skiing at high speeds. The accelerating thrust of the downhill ski on weight transfer should not be allowed to push the ski sideways. This thrust is also more effective if immediately preceded by a slight lowering of the body. For acceleration to be possible, the thrust must be in

A study of the technique of Marc Giradelli in Todtnau

line with the body's centre of gravity and the direction of travel. If you raise your arms too high, or even stretch the body too much, this will cancel out the accelerating effect of the thrust. Aerodynamics and guiding technique are also very important in the giant slalom, but we shall not consider these in detail until we come to the downhill. Suffice to say that for erodynamic reasons the giant slalom enerally requires a somewhat lower ody position.

Stepping with uphill scissor is the sual technique in the giant slalom, ut this can in certain circumstances e varied. Sometimes there is simply ot enough time or space for an uphill cissor, in which case it can be nodified to parallel open stemming or phill stemming. The various eight-transfer techniques can also e combined with pressure turns (see page 69), in which the skis are turned in weighted rather than in unweighted state. Skiers have occasionally even been known to use step turns with downhill scissor, especially when a swing has been difficult to steer effectively or has been suddenly interrupted. The downhill ski should not be angled too far in such cases, or else the thrust — and hence the acceleration — will no longer be attainable.

Swing steering can be modified using a certain amount of rotation (see page 77). Note, however, that only the arms and upper body should be turned in the direction of the swing — never the hips, which should be left in their normal position.

Exaggerated edging and weighting of the outer ski

Tactics in giant slalom

Tactics in the giant slalom are fairly easy to describe, as far as optimum use of technique is concerned: you should brake no more than absolutely necessary, and accelerate as much as possible. To achieve this you should make the swings as rounded and as smooth as you can. This may be quite simple in theory, but it is a different matter trying to plan them so that your route runs through the gates. The swings must be so organised in relation to the positions of the gates that they pass smoothly between them without any sudden turns being necessary. You must plan your route a long way ahead, especially in relation to those gates which signal a new rhythm in the swings or a change of terrain. Even when a sequence of gates can be negotiated using only one type of swing, the radius and the length of the swings must still be carefully modified so as to make them as smooth and as round as possible. If braking is at all necessary, then it should only be done either during or immediately before a steep section. Braking before or during a shallow section will lose you too much valuable time. Giant-slalom technique should be modified as follows, depending on the circumstances which apply:

● Steep terrain:
  ○ step turns with open parallel stemming or uphill stemming
  ○ stick planting during swing

● Shallow terrain:
  ○ stepping with pressure turns
  ○ ski as smoothly as possible
  ○ no stick planting during swing

● Hard, icy *piste*:
  ○ no rotation in steering
  ○ stepping with pressure turns

● Soft, often rutted *piste*:
  ○ some rotation in steering

● Sections with sharp turns:
  ○ consciously steer with the skis, and avoid letting them skid sideways
  ○ try to gain height when stepping

● Smooth, fast sections:
  ○ relatively low body posture
  ○ ski in as straight a line as possible

Given the length of the giant slalom course, it is especially likely to cause problems of fatigue. Breathe deeply and deliberately, and match your breathing to the physical effort involved. This will help you to conserve oxygen over the whole length of the race. Have a good look at the course beforehand. Try to work out the best route from the point of view of rhythm and terrain, and see if there are any sequences of gates which might possibly be taken in one swing.

Super-giant slalom

The 1982/83 season saw the addition of a new competition to World Cup skiing: the super-giant slalom, also known as "super G" or "giant slalom in one run". The race seems to have become firmly established in the skiing programme, although it is still a matter of some debate. The super-giant slalom is laid out in one single course, and technically it lies somewhere between the giant slalom and the downhill. It is characterised by higher speeds and larger swing radii than the giant slalom, and the race should also include two jumps. The height difference, too, is greater than that of the giant slalom. We shall not give any specifications here, as there are still likely to be some changes. It has so far been included in the programme at the expense of the normal giant slalom, which has rightly been seen as an unjustified attack on the status of the classical discipline. Several important persons are trying to get the authorities to grant it the status of a discipline alongside slalom, giant slalom and downhill. No doubt it will eventually have its own small band of specialists who will fight to maintain its status. This could be seen as yet another nail in the coffin of all-round expertise. As it is, the men's sport already consists almost exclusively of single-discipline specialists. Perhaps the best chance for the super-giant slalom would be a combined competition for specialists from all three of the classical disciplines. The super-giant slalom requires a high level of specific conditioning and involves techniques whch are used in both the giant slalom and the downhill. They have even begun to develop special super-G skis, which are superficially not unlike those used in the downhill. Time alone will show what is to become of this new discipline, and what new potential it contains.

A spectacular moment in the downhill — crowning glory of the Alpine disciplines

Downhill

What is downhill?

There are a number of basic requirements for the downhill course. It must, for example, be possible to ski the whole length of the course without any help from stick planting or pushing. More than that, the course should not contain any large bumps. Jumps which land on a shallow or diagonal slope are to be avoided. The route is marked out by means of eight-metre-wide gates, which are used to indicate dangerous points in the course, to reduce the speed in very fast stretches, and to define the route which the skier should take. There should always be a wide enough safety zone on either side of the track, in which obstacles such as trees, rocks or lift poles are protected by padding or netting. A modern downhill *piste* might easily be compared with a Formula 1 race track. The specifications are as follows:

- Height difference between the start and the finish:
  500–700 metres for women
  800–1000 metres for men

- Time specifications at the Winter Olympics:
  A best time of around 1 minute 40 for women
  A best time of around 2 minutes for men

The number of gates is not actually specified, and depends on what the gates are needed for, whether for speed control or for safety. In the downhill, the body has to be kept in the typical downhill position for long stretches at a time, which means that good muscular endurance is absolutely essential, particularly in the legs — though it is less a question of staying in one position than is often imagined, as the posture must continually be adjusted to compensate for the many irregularities in the track. Muscular endurance in the legs is similarly needed to cope with long curves by providing steady resistance to the centrifugal effects of turning. This muscular endurance must be built up on a solid basis of muscular power in the legs. The forces to be reckoned with when landing from jumps, or when dealing with awkwards bumps and turns in the course, can often amount to as much as five times the body weight. This means that all muscles in the body must be fully developed in order to protect the spine and joints from any possible jarring or injury.

There are a number of techniques which are of particular importance in the downhill. A downhill skier must be in full command of all the cornering and gliding techniques, and in particular that of skiing in the downhill position. Compensation technique must also be sufficiently developed to cope with jumps of as much as forty metres in length. The equipment can often make all the difference between winning and losing. The gliding ability of the skis and the aerodynamic qualities of the clothing are the decisive factors here. The downhill also requires enormous resources of courage and determination, particularly on difficult courses such as the one at Kitzbühel. For the downhill contains a not inconsiderable element of risk. Perhaps it is this which has aroused such incredible interest and enthusiasm among the spectators of this most popular and spectacular of the Alpine disciplines.

Layout of the Kandahar men's downhill course in Garmisch-Partenkirchen

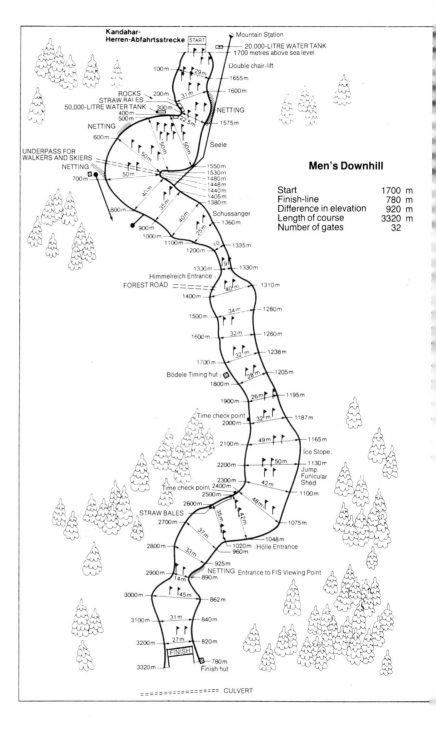

Men's Downhill

Start	1700 m
Finish-line	780 m
Difference in elevation	920 m
Length of course	3320 m
Number of gates	32

Technique in downhill

A versatile technique is important for the downhill, but is less decisive from a performance point of view than in the slalom or giant slalom. Technical loopholes can in fact be compensated for by good equipment and determination on the part of the racer.

The negotiation of fast, smooth curves is the first element of downhill skiing. The actual technique involved is not unlike the swing technique in the giant slalom. The outer ski should be heavily weighted during the

open stemming is better here. The exaggerated vertical movement so characteristic of the giant slalom should be considerably reduced when dealing with bends in the downhill. The chief function of vertical movement in the downhill is to compensate for irregularities in the course. If the snow is soft, the skis are often more evenly weighted during the steering phase of the swing. This disturbs the snow less and allows the skis to glide better. The body should be held in a crouching position, even

in performance. Gliding technique can be defined as the ability to keep the friction between the skis and the snow to an absolute minimum. For this to be possible, the movement and weighting of the skis must be finely adjusted to every change or unevenness in the course. The best gliding is achieved when there is no edging at all and the skis are completely flat on the snow.

At speeds of over 80 kilometres per hour, aerodynamics has a very important effect on performance. The

Jumping over an edge and negotiating a bend in the downhill

steering phase of the swing. The swing is normally introduced by means of a step turn with parallel open stemming. The use of uphill stemming does not provide for any more acceleration at the high speeds involved, which means that parallel

on the bends, so as to keep wind resistance to a minimum. The arms are held well forwards to help balance the body. On bends, the inner hand is held in front of the outer hand, to help balance the cornering position at the high speeds involved.

But the downhill involves more than just negotiating bends. Gliding technique is a far more decisive factor

laws of aerodynamics are not easy to understand, as they depend on so many different factors. Wind resistance is determined by the cross-sectional area of the body which is moving against the wind. Another important factor is the drag caused by the turbulence which is built up. Note, however, that aerodynamic considerations should never be allowed to interfere with gliding or swing technique. Given that stipulation, the following principles should be observed:

● Wind resistance should be kept to a minimum by presenting as small an area of the body as possible; this can be achieved by:
  ○ keeping the body down
  ○ holding the arms in front
  ○ pushing the shoulders forwards
● Turbulence should also be kept to a minimum by:
  ○ keeping the back rounded, maybe even slightly humped
  ○ keeping the legs well apart
  ○ keeping the arms well out if they are not in front

There is a crouching position which is typical of the downhill. It combines all the elements which have been dealt with so far with regard to gliding technique and aerodynamics. The downhill *crouch* (or *tuck*) can be described as follows:

● Keep the skis flat and well apart.
● Weight the skis evenly.
● Keep the angle of the knees at approximately 90 degrees (not less), or else the muscles will become too heavily loaded and will tire much too quickly.
● Bend over until your chest is just above your thighs, and so that your head and the hump of your rounded back form a line which is parallel to the ground.
● Hold your hands in front of your face, with your elbows immediately in front of your knees.

continued on page 126

Steve Podborski at the famous Hundschopf leap in Wengen

The downhill position is in some ways an uncomfortable one, but it should become natural and relaxed for the downhill skier, and should allow for sufficient leg movement to ensure that the skis can glide effectively.

A technique must also be developed for skiing over an edge into one of those well-known jumps. Jumps are not likely to make any difference to the timing, but bad technique can lead to dangerous falls. Observe the following points when jumping:

● Choose a good approach route.
● Raise your body slightly on approaching the edge.
● Immediately before the edge, lower your body to the extent that the circumstances demand, in order to prepare for the jump.
● Remain in this position throughout the jump, taking special care not to raise your upper body.
● Land as softly as possible on flat skis.

Good jumping technique requires courage, determination and a keen awareness of the terrain.

Good downhill technique will considerably lessen the degree of risk involved, both during training and in the race itself, thus ensuring that your skiing career will be both a long and a successful one.

Tactics in downhill

Like other disciplines, the downhill offers a vast number of different possibilities, the correct choice of which can determine the outcome of the race. However, on certain parts of the course the choice is limited and depends very much on the terrain. There are, for instance, long stretches for which the downhill crouch is the only appropriate technique, while other sections might consist of one

jump after another interspersed with dangerous bends. The tactical possibilities are infinitely varied, but there are a number of general principles which may be of help:

● The route:
  ○ Choose the route from the start to the finish which is quickest for you.
● The character of the track:
  ○ While training on course, try to determine those sections in which the most time can be won or lost. Then, as you analyse your performance, make a special note of these key points in the course.
● Steep terrain:
  ○ Take full advantage of the extra acceleration.
  ○ Concentrate on a good aerodynamic posture.
  ○ The decreased friction between the skis and the snow means that gliding technique is no longer of such paramount importance.
● Shallow terrain:
  ○ Glide as perfectly as you can.
  ○ Do not allow aerodynamic considerations to interfere with your gliding technique.
● Broad curves:
  ○ Keep your swings even and regular.
  ○ Steer carefully through the swings without skidding.
  ○ Keep your body position as low as you can without adversely affecting the swing (crouching will make the skis skid sideways).
● Narrow bends:
  ○ Make an exact assessment of the route you are about to take.
  ○ Exaggerate the weighting of the outer ski during the swing itself.
  ○ Hold the inner hand well ahead of the outer hand as you move through the swing.

  ○ Concentrate on swing technique over and above everything else.

There are a lot more suggestions we could make regarding special situations which might arise. But tactics could best be summed up as follows: familiarise yourself with every aspect of the course as much as you possibly can, and try to work out how much risk you can afford to take in the specific circumstances on the basis of your own individual technique, motivation, determination and courage. But while concentrating on tactics, do not forget to make sure that your equipment is in tip-top condition. Only with the very best equipment can you expect to give of your best and produce a really good result.

The personality of the Alpine racer

Throughout the history of Alpine racing, outstanding skiers have left their own personal stamp on whatever disciplines they have followed. Every new competitor is measured against them, and no race is decided until the stars have completed the course. What are we to conclude from this? Have these top sportsmen learned some special trick? Of course not! All the different elements which make up their performance, whether it be technical ability, tactical knowledge or physical fitness, are ultimately bound up with their individual personalities. Top sportsmen belong to a very specific type. Most of them, for example, are blessed with a terrific will-power, which influences everything they do. It enables them to be fully in control of their emotions, so that absolutely everything is geared towards that one goal of success and of winning the next race. This incredible will-power is sometimes quite obvious, though they are often very clever at covering it up.

A large part of this will-power consists of a deep motivating conviction. The motivation to succeed must be more than just a flash in the pan: it must be sustained throughout the sportsman's career, both in training and in competition. Only a deep inner "calling" is sufficient to withstand the stresses which are involved. External motivations such as money and travel are never enough in the end. After all the inevitable sacrifices, disappointments and defeats, something from inside is needed to be able to plunge back into training and competition with the same enthusiasm as before.

The true sportsman also possesses a special kind of intelligence, which enables him to observe and analyse how the sport functions and then to use this knowledge to improve his own performance. To do this he must first be keenly aware of his own feelings, and of his individual strengths and weaknesses. The ultimate object of this analysis must be to use his strengths to their full advantage, and to reduce and eradicate his weaknesses.

Many of our most outstanding sportsmen have an almost unshakeable belief in their own personal success. Even at moments of failure, they remain firmly convinced of their abilities and of the fact that success is just round the corner. Such conviction is born of self-confidence and unwavering hope for the future.

Yet however much a sportsman's success is based on the right temperament and a positive attitude towards the sport, there is always a certain amount of luck involved, which ensures their success at those decisive moments in the competition.

The number who reach the top is naturally very few. And yet, however well or badly your own sporting career might turn out, there is much in it which will be of benefit to you in later life. As you get older you will only remember the good times, and the unpleasant experiences will be forgotten. So the best of luck with your racing career!

Toni Sailer

Franz Klammer

Jean-Claude Killy

Ingemar Stenmark

"On the snow" training plan

This is often known as snow training, though the term is somewhat misleading, as it is the skier who must train and not the snow. Training is one of the most important aspects of Alpine racing. You will already be familiar with the principles of a training plan from the section on planning a conditioning programme (see page 104). The programme must first be based on a set of aims and objectives. Think carefully about what are your greatest strengths and weaknesses and build your training programme around them. But at the same time, note that there are some general principles which might be observed when planning your programme:

● First practise your general skiing technique on the open slope: for example, broad and narrow swings, all the various types of weight transfer, and gliding steering in the swing.
● Then go on to practise more specific techniques, again on the open slope: for example, slalom swings and giant slalom swings in different terrains and snow conditions.
● After this, continue to practise these techniques, but in runs which are specifically intended for them.
● Once you have fully mastered these techniques, start training as if you were in the race proper, taking full account of all the tactical considerations which apply to the particular discipline.
● Even during the races themselves, keep a weather eye out for any

technical defects, and try to eliminate them immediately using specific technical exercises. Your results can only be as good as your technique.
● As with condition training, correct timing is of the essence. Plan your programme carefully from the point of view of both the amount and the intensity of training.

Below is an example of a skier's training programme for a whole year. It consists of a suggested training programme for someone who plans to compete in all three disciplines in the winter season. Like the conditioning programme on page 105, it is for a skier of between 15 and 24 years of age who has not yet reached the national squad, and who has little opportunity for skiing during the summer or early autumn.

A skiing training schedule

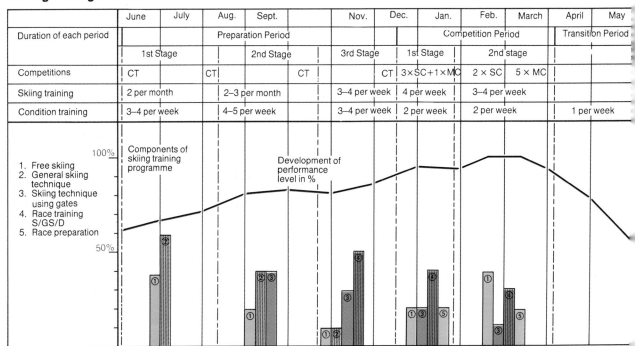

	June	July	Aug.	Sept.		Nov.	Dec.	Jan.	Feb.	March	April	May
Duration of each period		Preparation Period							Competition Period		Transition Period	
	1st Stage			2nd Stage		3rd Stage	1st Stage		2nd stage			
Competitions	CT		CT		CT		CT	3×SC+1×MC	2 × SC	5 × MC		
Skiing training	2 per month			2–3 per month		3–4 per week	4 per week		3–4 per week			
Condition training	3–4 per week			4–5 per week		3–4 per week	2 per week		2 per week		1 per week	

Components of skiing training programme

Development of performance level in %

1. Free skiing
2. General skiing technique
3. Skiing technique using gates
4. Race training S/GS/D
5. Race preparation

Key to abbreviations ► CT = Condition test
► SC = Secondary competitions
►MC = Main competitions

Luck

(as told by Rosi)

The Germans have a saying that luck always seeks out its own kind. Is that why I was lucky in Innsbruck? At first sight that might well seem to have been the case, in that everything went right at the same time: the weather, the course, the skis, my health, and all the rest. But the performance depends on every little detail. For luck to achieve much, it must be supported by the desire to do everything properly, and to be so well prepared that when the crunch comes you can say to yourself, "Well, I've done everything I possibly can — I'm fully equipped!"

If you've written things down in your training book which you never did, merely in order to impress your coach (which is ultimately no more than self-deception), then you don't really deserve any luck. Those were the sort of childish tricks which I got up to, though I can hardly credit it these days. It was only when I stopped playing around and began to concentrate properly on my sport that "luck" really began to turn my way.

I don't wish to sound arrogant, but I can tell you that the medals I won in Innsbruck were no mere stroke of luck; they were the product of hard work and effort. Life, after all, is what you make it.

But what about the spate of bad luck which I had had previously? Was it merely due to bad preparation? There are several examples I could mention.

The first was at the start of the giant slalom at Sapporo, when the zip in my over-trousers suddenly got caught. What a to-do there was!

"Somebody get me a knife!" roared my trainer Klaus Mayr. Things were sorted out in the nick of time, but the damage was done. I was in such a state of nerves that I lost valuable time.

Again in Sapporo, I was in the bus on my way to the downhill when the baskets on my sticks got caught in the heater and melted into strange spherical objects. A few years later, someone invented a similar spherical device to replace the traditional basket. Maybe the idea had come from me! In Japan it was no new invention as far as I was concerned, but merely a problem I could have done without.

Yet again, at the Olympics in Sapporo, we were warming ourselves up in the tents at the start of the slalom. I had my skiing goggles wrapped around my arm, and I must have stood too near the heater. The result was that the lenses were badly buckled. But again, in the nick of time I managed to find a replacement — from the rival firm, what is more.

The next disaster was in 1973, at the World Cup in Sterzing: this time I simply *had* to "pay a call" — but where? There wasn't a single tree in sight, but I managed to struggle onto a cornice above the starting area. The cornice collapsed and carried me several yards downhill. No one had seen me, so I struggled back up again, and arrived at the start just before the whistle. But by this time I was frozen stiff and my hands were numb. I came off course at the first gate, which was only to be expected in the circumstances.

Finally in 1974, at the World Cup in St Moritz, I managed to ruin one of my boots while training for the giant slalom, which meant that I had to race in a pair of brand new boots.

And that was not all that happened in St Moritz. I was doing marvellously in the downhill when my bindings sprang open of their own accord and I fell.

At such times it feels as if the world has come to an end, especially in an international competition. However, it taught me how to cope with defeat, and also how to learn from it.

I was dogged by disaster from 1972 to 1974, but was this merely a question of bad luck? Hardly. Most of the mishaps were due to poor concentration and lack of preparation. And was it merely a question of good luck when I won in Innsbruck in 1976? Again, no. By this time I had learnt to concentrate — a process which had begun in 1974 and had taken two years to develop. But how lucky it was that I had chosen the right two years in which to do this!

From child to adult racer

Written in collaboration with Heinz Mohr,
coach in charge of junior training,
German Skiing Federation

Ask any young skier what he wants to be when he grows up, and the answer will be "A skier like Stenmark or Klammer." All of them want to ski like their idols — to wedel gracefully between the gates, to streak down the track at breakneck speed, and to taste the glory of victory.

The road to victory is a long one, with many sacrifices on the way. But children should still be encouraged to ski. It is such a wonderful sport; and a solid grounding in skiing, at whatever level, is an invaluable training for any other type of sport. Neither is it necessary to aim for the top. It is enough to be able to master the sport and to enjoy it for its own sake. The important thing, however, is for parents, teachers and coaches to be fully aware of the developmental processes involved, and to take full account of these as they teach the children to ski.

It is for this reason that we offer you some words of advice, on the basis of recent knowledge on the subject, and of our own personal experience.

The long process of transforming children into adult skiers has been divided into four stages on the basis of the technical requirements of Alpine skiing and of the children's physical emotional development:

1 Elementary training
   From 3 to 9
2 Foundation training
   From 10 to 13
3 Performance training
   Boys: from 14 to 18
   Girls: from 13 to 16
4 High-performance training
   Boys: from 18 onwards
   Girls: from 16 onwards

Each of these stages contains a number of specific training objectives. These should be carefully noted and strictly observed, as the effect of training varies enormously, depending on what stage of emotional and physical development the child has reached.

It is also extremely important to build up the training on the basis of what has already been covered, right down to the smallest detail. The courses are designed to merge with one another, which means that the ages given are to a certain extent arbitrary.

Children's skiing

Alpine skiing is technically very demanding, so it is essential to develop the various motor abilities from an early age. The learning of the basic movement not only makes for greater technical refinement in the more advanced stages of training, but also produces healthier children generally.

Even before he goes to school, the child will begin to show a strong

A little Franz Klammer — on the road to fame

131

feeling for movement and an interest in motor activity. It is important at this early age to kindle the curiosity of the child and awaken his interest in sport, by encouraging him in a variety of activities and experiences of a physical nature. Such play can come in a number of different forms. Playing in the snow, for example — building snowmen, snowball fights, sliding, tobogganing — will help familiarise the child with the winter environment and encourage him to enjoy the snow.

Parents who have high hopes for their chidren's skiing should note that such play is essential if the child is to become really interested. Skiing does not always come naturally to young children. Only positive experiences will arouse their interest, thus ensuring that they do not develop an aversion to the sport.

If after this initial stage of familiarisation the child is beginning to show a keen interest, he can then begin to learn a few of the elementary skiing techniques and try them out in a variety of simple situations. A good way of doing this is to enrol the child in a children's course at a ski school. The teaching here is serious in purpose but informal in method. The teachers are specially trained to teach children to ski in a way which is compatible with their physical and motor development.

The parents and teachers should note the following:

- The child must be introduced to skiing in an environment which is natural to him.
- Exercises and instruction should be presented in a spirit of play, and there should be no sense of compulsion. At the same time, do not keep lifting, carrying or holding the child in a vain attempt to improve his balance; let him work it out for himself.
- Young children find it difficult to concentrate for very long, and their

minds are continually on the move. You should therefore be constantly presenting them with exciting and imaginative things to do.

The first years at school are marked by a dramatic development in the child's motor abilities. If sporting activities are presented in an interesting way, children are amazingly enthusiastic and eager to learn. The pleasure of movement is soon accompanied by a genuine desire to achieve. There are two things in particular which you should take into account. Firstly, the child will be hungry for activity, and this need must be met by providing him with as many different sporting opportunities as possible. The aim is for him to develop a whole variety of skills, so that even some of the apparently difficult techniques will

become relatively easy to master. Secondly, the desire to achieve must be further encouraged by playful competition with other children of the same age. Even at this young age, it is vital for children to build up a strong motivation and a sense of achievement.

One important aspect of training children to ski is to introduce them to the varied terrain and conditions of the *piste*. This provides a wonderful opportunity to teach them all the elementary techniques, for even at this early stage children can begin to find ways of coping with different situations. Experience has shown that even young children are quite capable of understanding the need for a variety of techniques, provided they are first introduced to a variety of different situations.

Obstacle courses are a marvellous way of encouraging children to compete against one another. It is possible, for example, to create simple slalom courses which require a variety of swing techniques. Skiing off the *piste* is yet another exciting form of adventure.

Other games and activities are also good for developing general fitness: for example, simple gymnastics to improve physical skills, and ball games to improve agility and reaction time. Such activities are easy to introduce at this stage if the children are given plenty of choice in the matter. Rosi and her sister Evi were especially lucky in being brought up close to nature on the Winklmoosalm. They played in the woods every day, and went for long mountain hikes with their father. This was a marvellously natural way of developing their general physical skills.

Note the following:

- The training should always be presented in a varied and interesting way.
- The child's efforts should be constantly rewarded by positive enouragement and praise. Even when he has performed a technique wrongly, he should at least be praised for his courage, application and enthusiasm.
- Teachers and coaches should always carefully demonstrate the techniques and exercises which they ask the children to do. The children's desire to imitate means that the visual element is particularly significant at this age.

Foundation training

This particular stage of the child's development is often described as "the best age for learning", or the age when he "learns everything at the first attempt". But learning at this age is by no means automatic; it is rather based on the training which has already gone before. Only if a solid basis of varied skills has already been achieved during the initial stages will the child's motor development reach its full potential at a later stage. But once you have reached the point where techniques can be "learned in one go" — and this usually happens between the ages of 10 and 13 — the task remains to steer and control these skills in the most appropriate way.

Speed and agility also improve at this stage, as a result of a sudden boost in the level of physical fitness.

These favourable developments provide the ideal circumstances for beginning a systematic programme of skiing training. Training should be structured on the basis of four main objectives:

1 Refinement of the whole range of techniques specific to skiing
2 During the summer season, further training in motor and co-ordinative skills by means of alternative sporting activities.
3 A carefully-planned programme of general fitness training, later to be increasingly supplemented by specific conditioning.
4 Some participation in competitions, so that those skills which have been acquired may be tested in a competitive situation.

The programme is thus primarily one of general technical training. Those techniques which are basic to all types of skiing should become so ingrained and automatic that they cannot later be unlearned. The coach must therefore have a very clear idea of what he is setting out to achieve. And since the child is by now starting to think logically and methodically, he should also be given the reasons for the techniques he is learning.

The basic elements of technique have already been fully covered in previous chapters. They are:

- *Body posture*: The achievement of a *neutral state*, which can be sensed through the soles of the feet and can be readily adjusted to the changing circumstances. Children often show a marked tendency to lean back too far, which should be eliminated at all costs. It is also vitally important for the boots to fit correctly, and to allow for sufficient movement and play in the ankles.
- *Weighting the outer ski* by correctly aligning the hip during swing steering. Children tend to twist the upper body in the opposite direction (torsion position), and this should be discouraged.
- *Vertical movement* in the ankles, knees and hips for the purposes of weighting and unweighting. Note, however, that properly weighted skiing requires well-developed thigh muscles.
- *Stick planting:* The sticks should be held with the arms only slightly bent, and away from and in front of the body. Many children tend to let their sticks hang loose from their hands, and to forget to plant them.

Training should still be conducted mainly while skiing on the open slope. The disciplines of slalom, giant slalom and downhill should be gradually introduced into the routine, but only for the purpose of improving the skiing technique generally.

Training for slalom and giant slalom

The course should be carefully planned as a combination of runs and sequences of gates which encourages the child to refine and develop the basic techniques. It should therefore include a whole variety of broad and narrow swings, of steep and shallow gradients, and of soft and hard *piste*.

But all courses should have one thing in common: they should never require the child to turn or brake sharply, but instead should encourage him to develop a fluid, rhythmic and dynamic technique.

Training for downhill

Because of their readiness to take risks and their enormous agility, children should indeed be encouraged to practise the downhill, but on a special children's course.

Such training will boost their confidence at high speeds, and will improve their gliding and jumping skills. Experience has shown that children like the downhill most of all. And this enjoyment can often create a long-lasting attachment to this most spectacular of the disciplines (though

at this stage slalom and giant slalom should be taught at the same time).

For this reason, it is very much worth the extra work and effort involved in preparing a downhill course for children. (The necessary safety procedures make this a decidedly daunting task.)

Physical training

Regular fitness training is an essential concomitant to training in skiing techniques.

The chief object of fitness training at this stage is to improve the body's general fitness and specifically to develop the thigh muscles. Without this the skiing technique can never be practised effectively. The best forms of training for this are acrobatic activities such as trampolining, gymnastics and the martial arts, together with skiing-type exercises such as angled hops, crouch jumps and slalom runs.

Hints on the training programme

By now the child is beginning to develop intellectually, and will soon start to make criticisms about the content and structure of the training programme. It is important at this stage to sustain his interest in the sport by providing as much factual information as possible, and also by encouraging him to be self-critical.

From this point onwards, it is absolutely essential to extend the training programme by gradually increasing both the amount and the intensity of training. The programme should be carefully planned and prepared for the whole year, taking full account of seasonal changes and interruptions such as holidays.

A further word about competitions

Children have a great need for an objective means of assessing their progress, and this can to a large extent be met by taking part in small competitions. However, parents and coaches who are too ambitious will tend to over-emphasise the importance of objective performance levels. The result of this will be too much emphasis on racing technique and on one or two specific disciplines. Basic technical faults will often go unnoticed, and will be extremely difficult to correct at a later stage.

Competitive skiing should therefore be introduced in small doses, and should never be regarded as the only criterion of assessment.

The time is long overdue for the various skiing organisations to take a long, hard look at the present system of children's and junior competitions, and to set about restructuring them on the basis of modern developmental knowledge.

Performance training

Many readers will be worried by the use of the term "performance training" with reference to children between the ages of 13 and 16. For up until recently, puberty has been seen as a time of physical and emotional crisis. Doctors have advised adolescents to keep away from competitive sport, and occasionally even to avoid sport altogether.

However, modern research has provided incontrovertible evidence that puberty is a time in which a person's physical capabilities are markedly increased. Provided that adolescents have been adequately prepared in earlier years, their performance will continue to make steady progress.

If the physical and motor abilities are to become sufficiently developed to provide a basis for later high-

performance training, it is essential to embark on a serious programme of performance training at this stage. It is, however, vitally important to choose a method of training which take full account of the anatomical changes, in particular that of skeletal growth, which take place during puberty. Failure to do so can lead to serious physical damage. The enormous growth spurt which is so well known in puberty will often have an adverse effect on technique. The sudden changes in the skeletal proportions produce a characteristic clumsiness, which limits the possibilities of technical inprovement and can sometimes cause problems with techniques which have already been learned. For this reason the following

aspects of training should be particularly emphasised:

● Technical training towards the consolidation of those techniques which have already been mastered.
● More advanced general fitness training as a continuation of what has already been achieved, plus the further development of those specific skills which are essential to performance.
● A marked increase in both the amount and the intensity of training.
● Regular participation in competitions, which should match the standard which the young person has reached.

continued on page 138

Age-group	Training Objectives	Training Content	Practical Tips
Pre-school years **approx. 4–6 years**	ENJOYMENT OF MOVEMENT AND PLAY — both generally and in the snow To awaken an interest in sport, and in winter sports in particular ● development of a variety of motor skills, especially flexibility ● familiarity with winter conditions ● some training in children's skiing	Imaginative structuring of play, involving a variety of motor activities: ● obstacle courses ● games, including ball games ● family gymnastics ● open-air games in the countryside ● games such as tag or hide-and-seek ● skating and tobogganing ● building snowmen ● snowball fights ● making patterns with skis in the snow ● elementary skiing exercises on a gentle slope	The best kinds of games for this age-group are those without winners or losers Note the following: ● warm, dry clothing ● stop when they have had enough ● plenty of variety ● tasks which can be carried out in a spirit of play
Early years at school **approx. 7–9 years**	VARIED BUT STRUCTURED TRAINING — both generally and in the snow Wide and varied experience in a large number of different sporting activities ● development of co-ordination ● improvement of speed and reaction time ● basic training in skiing techniques	A wide variety of sporting activities, such as tennis, swimming, and other competitive games ● gymnastics ● trampolining ● children's games (hide and seek, tag, sack races, relay racing, etc.) Training in all the basic forms of swing technique, including: ● a variety of terrains and snow conditions ● slalom and obstacle courses ● skill exercises, such as one-legged skiing, skiing without sticks, ski-jumping and shadow skiing	These skill exercises are particularly good as a form of basic training Exercise should be kept within limits and interspersed with frequent rests to avoid overburdening the system Note the following points of method: ● visual demonstration is always extremely effective ● a varied programme will ensure good all-round training ● children love to compete amongst themselves ● keep the gates close together and near to the fall line ● every training session should include skill exercises
10–13 years old	BASIC TRAINING **Skiing training** Refinement of the basic skiing techniques Specific co-ordination training	Varied technical training ● controlled skiing on the open slope in a whole variety of situations ● training in the slalom and giant slalom with special emphasis on technique ● a course involving a whole series of different techniques: slalom — schussing — moguls; slalom — step turns — giant slalom; and so on ● downhill training over a large number of different kinds of terrain ● an even greater variety of skill exercises: fuzzy swings, step turns, one-legged slalom, or even doing a Charleston on the inner ski	Training should be carried out in all snow and weather conditions, even in very difficult conditions (powder snow, icy piste, moguled piste, etc.) Be sure to incorporate ● smooth, rhythmic runs with two poles to each gate ● a variety of different runs with broad and narrow swings ● use of two to three small flags for training the judgement and skiing of the right line Ensure in particular ● that you have taken all possible safety precautions (preparing the piste and fencing off danger areas) ● that you choose a suitably safe and easy slope

Age-group	Training Objectives	Training Content	Practical Tips
10–13 years old	**General training** Further development of general co-ordination, speed and reaction time Development of the basic motor skills	*Skill:* ● competitive games such as football and volleyball ● basic athletic training ● acrobatic exercises ● balancing exercises ● training to improve reaction time *Endurance:* ● intensive relay racing ● relay skiing ● interval training using an endless relay ● cycle relays *Muscular endurance:* ● circuit training, medicine-ball relay and judo *Mobility:* ● a programme of gymnastics	A good way of getting the necessary training is to go to a sports centre or join a sports club A good proportion of the skill and mobility exercises should be directly relevant to skiing, such as: ● angled hops (both one- and two-legged) ● slalom runs (both downhill and on the flat) ● jumping into crouch position (see page 107)
Boys: 14–18 years Girls: 13–16 years	PERFORMANCE TRAINING **Skiing training** Consolidation of the techniques so far achieved An increase in the amount of training undertaken Regular participation in competitions Refinement of the individual skier's abilities	*General technique:* ● controlled skiing on the open slope *Specific technique:* ● increased training towards competition level in the slalom, giant slalom and downhill ● specific training in starting and finishing a race ● analysis and rectification of individual weaknesses in technique	Training should be carried out in all three disciplines so as to avoid over-specialisation Training runs should be kept relatively simple, whatever the discipline Continuous, uninterrupted skiing on the open slope improves those aspects of fitness which are specific to skiing Skiing in difficult weather conditions is a useful form of individual training
	General training Improvement of the general level of fitness Development of those areas of fitness which are specific to skiing performance	*Basic endurance:* ● jogging for up to 60 three times ● cycling minutes at a time a week ● swimming pulse rate: 150–170 ● interval runs of increasing speed ● skiing for up to 40 minutes, with changes in speed according to the terrain *General strength:* ● gymnastic exercises without equipment ● gymnastic exercises using a medicine ball ● circuit training using small extra weights (medicine balls or dumb-bells) *Skill training:* ● further training in acrobatics, balancing and reaction time *Anaerobic training of the thigh muscles:* ● uphill step-jumps ● circuit jumps using a medicine ball ● one-legged angled hops ● a series of different jumps and sprints *Muscular endurance:* ● step-ups onto a box using a sandbag or a weighted vest ● downhill slalom runs ● uphill cycle sprints ● squat stands against the wall	Running and co-ordination exercises are the best form of preparation for these (sideways jumps, running on the spot, skipping, lifting, hopping, and various combinations of all of them) These exercises should also help to strengthen those much-neglected neck, shoulder and back muscles Young people of this age should concentrate primarily on keeping up those skills which they have already acquired Take care to avoid overburdening the system The following exercises are dangerous: ● twisting or bending backwards using weights ● exercises involving too much bending, straddling or stretching

Technical training

The techniques which have been learned (see *Foundation training*, page 133) should be adapted to the physical changes of puberty by means of regular training in all three disciplines. One might almost say that skiing technique must grow to keep pace with the body.

Participation in competitions should be planned systematically, so that the skier can be trained in the dynamics of skiing, and can learn to cope with bad weather or adverse *piste* conditions. Specific training in the slalom, giant slalom and downhill should be correspondingly increased. But the course should still be laid out fairly simply, and should never be too long; it can be gradually modified to include sharper and sharper bends. This will help to improve both the steering of the outer ski and the tactical ability to find the shortest route between the gates.

But the training programme should continue to include a large amount of skiing which is free from the constraints of poles and flags, but in which the exercises are still carefully structured. This provides an opportunity to concentrate on specific techniques, and on ways of improving and refining them. Looking at Ingemar Stenmark today, one can tell that he still practises swings on the open slope, specifically in order to perfect reducing the degree of skid to a minimum.

Teenagers grow very fast, and this can often affect motor co-ordination, causing exaggerated movement of the limbs during the swing. Patience is required on the part of the coach, and it is not advisable for the person affected to enter more than a very few competitions. Such problems can be best overcome by frequent and varied technique practice on the open slope.

Physical training

A good general fitness programme is at least as important as skiing training at this stage. A varied programme of general conditioning will considerably enhance the process of growth and development. Specific conditioning should also be incorporated increasingly into the programme, so as to form a solid basis for the period of high-performance training which follows.

Endurance training

Skiing is not usually counted as an endurance sport, but endurance training is nonetheless vital at this stage as a solid basis for later high-performance training. Skiing can make heavy demands on the human system, both in the extreme climatic conditions (i.e. snow and ice) and in the intense physical activity involved. Aerobic endurance can be greatly improved at this stage by suitably developing the circulo-respiratory system. A systematic endurance programme is therefore of the utmost importance. This should include jogging, cycling or swimming throughout the preparation period (summer and early autumn). There should be at least three training sessions a week, each lasting up to an hour. During the session the pulse rate should lie somewhere between 150 and 170 (this will vary from person to person, and it is up to the coach to make an individual assessment). This should be preceded by a warm-up session which may consist of, for example, 20 minutes of running and co-ordination exercises.

Strength training

A programme of gymnastics, both with and without props, is by far the best method for the general strengthening of all the muscles of the body. This should be further supplemented by circuit training using small weights such as medicine balls and dumb-bells.

Extra training of certain specific groups of muscles is also required: namely those of the thighs, the stomach and especially the back. On the one hand they must be able to act and react very quickly; on the other hand they must be able to sustain heavy loads for as long as two minutes at a time. These specific strength capabilities can be developed by means of special exercises (see page 104). There are, for example, a number of special jumping and knee-bending exercises which develop these parts of the body in much the same way as skiing, whether in training or competitions. Such specific strength training is an essential basis for later technical perfection.

There are several forms of training which should be excluded from the specific training programme at this stage, as they are apt to overload the spine and knee joints, causing considerable damage. Strength exercises involving partners or heavy weights are therefore out, as is also isometric training.

General co-ordination

Other important requirements for Alpine skiing are agility, mobility and a fast reaction time. These abilities must be developed from childhood onwards if they are to reach their optimum potential. Even in the teenage years, they can quickly stagnate or even deteriorate if they are not constantly exercised and kept up to scratch.

It follows from this that general co-ordination is another important component of the general fitness-training programme. The best forms of co-ordination training at this stage are the various forms of gymnastic exercises, together with the acrobatic exercises which were already included in the foundation training programme. Only a very limited number of new exercises may be introduced at this stage.

Sports such as football, volleyball and basketball can also be extremely effective as a supplementary form of co-ordination training. Our own experience has shown how important is the competitive urge at this young age. A ball game can be a far more effective incentive to training than any amount of encouragement from a coach.

Some advice on the training programme

The biological age of the child can vary by as much as 18 months either way relative to his chronological age. The coach should be able to tell if a person is an early or late developer, so that the training programme can be adjusted accordingly.

● Performance in junior competitions often depends more on individual physical development than on technical ability. This should always be borne in mind when assessing the results.

● Training methods and the equipment used should be chosen extremely carefully at this stage. Overload in training can lead to hormone disturbances and irreparable skeletal damage. Training should be carried out under medical supervision.

● The event of leaving or changing school can often create conflicts for the young skier. The coach should act as an adviser here, and provide help towards solving these problems.

● Girls and boys show marked differences in the way they develop at this stage. A coach should always take this into account when planning a training programme.

Christian Orlainsky from Austria was a world-class skier by the age of 16

High-performance training

The transition from performance to high-performance training is a fairly simple process, and usually takes place when the skier is promoted from the junior squad to the national squads. By now his physical development is virtually complete, and the body has, to all intents and purposes, reached its full training capacity. From a psychological point of view, the skier has now reached the stage where he can achieve the total devotion to the sport which the hard training programme requires.

The aim of high-peformance training is for the individual skier to develop the highest possible level of performance in the slalom, the giant slalom or the downhill, and to strive to retain this level of performance for many years to come. This will necessarily involve training all the year round. The rhythm of the training should also be so organised that the skier will be in peak condition during the period in which most of the competitions take place. The training year should therefore be divided into specific periods, during which the skier should concentrate on certain particular forms of training.

Given that a sportsman can peak for only a short time, the programme must be so planned in years when the Winter Olympics and World Championships take place that he is able to peak as many as three times.

The first peak is often in the summer — which is why more and more countries are now able to send skiers to international events in New Zealand, Argentina and Australia.

The second high-point of the skiing year is in December at the time of the World Cup. At this point the skier should test his performance level, and improve his FIS points and starting position. Further condition training should then lead up to the highest peak of all, for the Winter Olympics or the World Championship. (In Innsbruck in 1976, Rosi managed to peak at exactly the right moment, which was the main reason why she was able to beat rivals who had previously beaten her.) The planning and content of the conditioning programme is the chief factor here. There are two very important points to bear in mind:

● The transition period, during which the body has had time to recover, should be followed by a period of improvement in the general level of fitness. The process should not, however, be a gradual one, but should rather take the form of short bursts of hard training.
● At such times the intensity of training is increased to an absolute maximum, to enable the sporting performance to peak the at the time required. This is yet another reason for planning the programme so as to produce three peaks, as any other form of programme always carries the danger of overtraining.

By now there is a considerable difference between the physical requirements of the slalom and giant slalom on the one hand, and of the downhill on the other. Quite apart from that, the international performance level has risen so enormously in recent years that only specialists have a chance of winning in the individual disciplines. This means that the content of the specific conditioning programme is very much determined by the particular discipline.

This is especially true of strength training. Downhill racers must now concentrate on developing the static strength in their thigh and trunk

By the age of 17, Rosi had reached the top starting group (the first 15 racers) in all three disciplines

muscles (isometric tests have shown that downhill skiers achieve higher scores in their thigh muscles than weight-lifters). Slalom and giant-slalom skiers, on the other hand, should concencrate on developing their dynamic strength.

Technical training at the high-performance level is a question of perfecting all the various techniques on the basis of one's individual capabilities. (Ingemar Stenmark's style is by no means suitable for everyone.) Skiing training is thus a continuous process of trying to achieve perfection, both in individual techniques and in competition situations. Here again, the different disciplines require an entirely different programme of training. All three of them have the same ultimate aim — that of achieving the shortest possible time — but:

● The **slalom** requires an explosive and flexible style of skiing. Swings should be so organised that they take the shortest possible route between the gates, and follow one another as quickly as possible. This is particularly true when flexible slalom poles are used.

● In the **giant slalom,** the swings must be so accurately routed and steered that the skis follow exactly the right path, with the minimum loss of speed.

● Perfect gliding is the prerequisite of the **downhill,** such that the friction between the skis and the snow is kept to an absolute mimimum. It also involves coping with a variety of bumps and curves at speeds of up to 85 miles per hour, without losing speed.

These techniques should be developed and perfected on the *piste*, in conditions which are as close as possible to those which apply in competition. Also, the more regularly you take part in important competitions, the more confident you will become from a psychological point of view. Your performance should always be at its best in competition, whatever the snow or weather conditions, and whatever stresses the competition itself might entail (for example, the Winter Olympics or the World Championships).

Apart from peak fitness and perfect technique, there is yet another important factor which determines performance, and that is the emotional attitude of the individual skier. Our own experience has shown that ultimate success depends on the best combination of all these three elements.

For most of our respective careers, we both achieved considerable success in the World Cup. But neither of us was able to achieve any stability in his or her performance, until our respective coaches at last managed to convince us that we would never

reach the top unless we concentrated our every effort on winning, by training as hard as we possibly could.

The coach plays yet another vital role, not just by providing the best possible training, but by encouraging the skier to adopt the right

Marc Giradelli in the slalom

professional attitude towards the sport.

It is the coach who shows him what to do, but it is up to the skier to carry this out.

Cars, cars and more cars

(as told by Christian)

I could write a whole book about skiers and their cars, because for some strange reason skiers all seem to be mad about cars. Downhillers in particular seem to love to indulge in a bit of rally-car racing. And most of them seem to have the same attitude to driving as to skiing: the faster the better!

On one occasion in 1974, after the Hahnenkamm slalom in Kitzbühel, I was driving unusually fast. I had won in Garmisch and Wengen, and I had been tipped as the favourite in Kitzbühel — but I had been beaten. The winner had been the Austrian Hansi Hinterseer. I was angry at losing, and I was in a hurry to get to the next port of call — which was probably why I was going "just a little bit" too fast on the road. The result was that I was stopped by the police near Wörgl and ordered to get out of the car.

"60 miles an hour!" roared the somewhat elderly policeman. "*And* in a built-up area! It was not long before we were joined by some of my World Cup cronies . . . I was feeling decidedly upset, and I was trying to explain my situation to the policeman. But he interrupted me with a smile: "My dear Mr Neureuther, because you were too slow on your skis today and Hansi overtook you, I'll allow that against your excessive driving speed! Would 100 *Schilling* be OK?

I could have hugged that policeman. And of course I paid up on the spot. The Swiss coaches had been caught for speeding too, but they were charged the full fine. They paid about

ten times as much for lesser offence — and so Austria got her own back on Switzerland, that other great skiing nation.

The Swiss Olympic champion Bernhard Russi could have done with a nice policeman like that when he was stopped on the Swiss *Autobahn* for driving at 120mph (the speed limit in Switzerland being 80mph). He was banned from driving on the spot, and had to walk home.

Wolfgang Junginger, who came third overall in the World Championship, had a similar experience when he was stopped by a policeman in Nördlingen. The policeman laughed and shook hands with him: "Radar trap! Congratulations! You're the fastest so far!" As a result he was banned from driving for six months.

There were no radar traps for me to worry about when I was invited to take part in the 1976 Scirocco Cup race on the Hockenheim Circuit. But alas, the race was a very short one. There was a three-car pile-up round the first bend, and mine was the fourth car to

join them. I looked round to see a fifth victim skidding towards me. The car was just about to hit mine when a brick on the track sent it flying. It sailed right over me and landed with a terrific crash, completely demolishing the three cars in front. The accident was so spectacular that it was dubbed the "crash of the year", and was shown on the New Year's Eve TV programme the following winter.

Even Rosi has tried her hand at motor racing. She had only just passed her test when she was invited to take part in a Formula 5 event on the famous Nürburg Circuit. Her luck was no better than mine. An inexperienced girl of 18, she drove straight into a fence — and out of the race. But in spite of that, the racing managers continued to invite her to take part in events. She never knew about this at the time, and later discovered that her parents, out of understandable concern for her welfare, had intercepted all their letters and phone-calls!

Maybe Rosi's parents had been put off by my own example. A few years

earlier, I had been on my way to see her when I drove my sports car off the road — whether from tiredness, impatience or yearning, I don't know — and performed a spectacular somersault. I walked on up to the house and whispered to Rosi that I had had an accident. "Please don't tell your parents", I begged her. But Rosi can never keep anything to herself, and rushed into the house to pass on the exciting news to her family — to her sisters in particular. Mr Mittermaier then came out to fetch my car out of the ditch.

My sports car was covered with dents, but to my relief it was still driveable. The next day I was driving back home to face the music. I was not very familiar with the road between Winklmoos and Garmsich — one of the routes of the ancient minnesingers — so I had no idea how dangerous the Maser Pass could be. I performed a pirouette and crashed into a rock face. the car was a complete write-off — though I had the compensation of a second evening with Rosi.

One of the most reckless drivers in the skiing world was Gerhard Prinzing, who came sixth overall in the 1968 Winter Olympics in Grenoble. He was on his way home from an event in France when he was stopped by the Swiss police. He had been driving pretty fast, so he knew he was in trouble. The policeman asked to see his driving license, so Gerhard showed him the document without actually giving it to him. The officer tried to take it from him, but he slapped him on the hand and said, "Don't take it, just look at it . . ." This of course landed him in the magistrates' court.

One evening Rosi and I were on our way home from a training course in Sölden. I was in a terrific hurry and stepped on the accelerator, much to Rosi's annoyance. And sure enough, I was stopped by the police in Telfs. I was still winding down the window when Rosi called out to the approaching policeman, "Now give him a really big fine! He's always going too fast!" There was no way I could get out of that one, so I simply paid up. But I was out of Austrian currency, so Rosi had to help me out.

To this day she has never had the money back again.

Competitive sport and its consequences

People are always asking me, "Christian, is it really worth all the trouble and effort which competitive sport involves these days?" And I always reply with an unqualified "Yes". Rosi is also of the opinion that we could never have found a more fulfilling occupation for our youthful years.

Competition was the magic formula that drove us on to do better, and we could have done nothing without it. I had no hesitation in giving up my university education, and I would have left school earlier if my parents had let me.

In my opinion, Rosi and I are no exceptions. All the competitive sportsmen we know think the same way as we do, and all of them find it extremely difficult when they are forced to give up. There are no particular financial incentives, because the sacrifices are usually greater than the rewards in all sports apart from those such as football. But in my opinion, even footballers would go on playing if the money were taken away. With slightly less enthusiasm, perhaps — but they would continue nonetheless!

There is that feeling of total fitness, and the sense of having completely mastered and perfected the sport. There is the tension and excitement of competition, and the glorious flush of success. There is the travelling, the camaraderie and the glory of fame — and there are new challenges around every corner. This alone is enough to persuade a sportsman to compete.

Alpine skiing offers such a variety of activities and opportunities. The chief training grounds are the mountain ranges: from the Alps to the Rockies, from New Zealand to the Andes.

Skiing does, however, suffer from one disadvantage, and one which very much limits the potential talent for the sport: the fact that very few people can practice it on their own doorstep. The best conditions for training are often only available at the cost of long journeys abroad.

But the popularity of the sport, together with the great commercial interest shown by the manufacturers, has meant that the sport has become continually more competitive over the years. If children or young people are to succeed as competitors, they must submit to an all-year-round programme of training. This means that their general education and professional studies will inevitably suffer.

The pyramid diagram overleaf will provide some further insight into the problem. Every year there are 15,000 West German children between the ages of 10 and 14 who take part in competitions run by ski clubs and schools. All of them are bouncing with enthusiasm and raring to go. Even at this early stage, the ski schools are beginning to channel them into serious training, and to teach them basic techniques which will make them excellent skiers for life. They are trained in groups, which teaches them

The Austrian Hansi Hinterseer at the professional championships in Aspen, USA

team spirit and to learn how to co-operate with one another. They must learn to put up with discomfort and inconvenience, and to sacrifice a number of more pleasurable activities, for the sake of their sporting ambitions. They must also learn to cope with success and failure.

These children are at the age when they are least certain of themselves, and are most likely to succumb to negative influences from outside. The educative influence of sport at this stage cannot be over-emphasised. Provided that parents do not push them too hard, by over-stressing the need for achievement, then the children will quickly develop an abiding interest in the sport, and will experience a sense of camaraderie which will go with them for the rest of their lives.

However, as the pyramid shows, of those 15,000 children only 500 are sufficiently talented or successful to be selected for further training. These 14- to 18-year-olds are divided into squads, and their training is geared towards a professional career.

18–22 years
30

14–18 years
500

10–14 years
15,000

The amount of time involved is then greatly increased. The summer and autumn are taken up with training, and the winter with competitions. From the age of 16, many of the most talented skiers take a special course to become World Cup skiers. Some of them may even take part in important national events.

This is also the stage at which the travelling begins. Young skiers in the squad must make long journeys to the various events both at home and abroad, which can mean that they are absent from school for weeks at a time. They thus run the risk of sacrificing a professional career for the sake of an uncertain future in sport.

Thank goodness there are so many understanding headmasters and teachers who are willing to make special provision for these children. It is thanks to them that our talent has not been lost to posterity, and that our national squad compares so well with that of East Germany. We are also very much indebted to our national sports centres, and to the opportunities provided by the military services, in which a sportsman has guaranteed employment when his sporting career is over.

A skier at this stage must never forget the high goal he is aiming for, especially in view of the fact that, of these 500 young skiers, only 30 will ever make it over the final hurdle into the national team.

Total dedication and optimum performance are demanded from this small group of professionals. The international standard is extremely high, and success is achieved at the cost of great sacrifice.

The statistics have shown that, of these 30 skiers in the national team, there are only two who make it right to the top. Only two out of the original 15,000 will actually get medals. Success and fame will mean that many doors are open for them, and

they will have few problems in carving out a career for themselves. For them it will certainly have been worth all the trouble. But what about all the others?

I personally am of the opinion that it is worth it for everyone. It is certainly an extremely satisfying feeling to be able to fulfil one's highest ambitions, but fame in sport is quickly forgotten. On the other hand, there is much more to sport than just that. If offers a whole range of experiences and activities, thus giving ample repayment for the "sacrifice" of a few years of one's youth. Indeed, those "lost years" of our youth were some of the most lively, interesting and enjoyable years of our lives.

Rosi and I were both lucky enough to have understanding parents, who helped and supported us in all our sporting aspirations. They gave us strength and security. We would like all children with sporting ambitions to have parents like ours. Then they, like us, will be able to agree with the French philosopher Henri de Montherlant (1896–1972), who said, "There is no time in youth which the mature person can look back on with as much happiness and gratitude as the time which he spent on the sports field!"

Drama in the snow

(as told by Rosi)

The winter of 1975/76 was a very worrying time for the team and the coaches, and also for my family. Not only were they concerned about my performance in the coming Winter Olympics, but there was a much worse problem: a blackmailer was threatening to kill me! It all started just before the event at St Gervais. I wasn't told about it af first, but I knew something was up. I kept noticing whispered conversations between my sister Evi and my coach Klaus Mayr. My father rang up and wanted to talk — but not to me — to Klaus, of all people! When we arrived at the hotel in Les Diablerets, I was booked into a different room from the one I was actually given — and so it went on.

At Berchtesgaden I was puzzled by the presence of two strangers who seemed to wander around during my training sessions. They were not exactly following me, but I kept seeing them at the hotel too.

Eventually Evi let me into the secret, but only after the matter had to a certain extent been settled. My sister Heidi, having first consulted with the police, had left 50,000 German Marks at a bus stop near Reit im Winkl. The blackmailer had not turned up; but some schoolchildren had found the case full of money, which they had handed in at the lost-property office.

But the surveillance continued in Innsbruck. There were several more murder threats after I won my first medal. I was given two rather nice policemen to protect me. They drove me around in their car, which was very comfortable and extremely interesting. Their walkie-talkie kept me fully informed as to the whereabouts of King Carl Gustav of Sweden, and the route which Chancellor Kreisky was taking to the ice stadium. The officers never actually called them by name. They used code words like "XY" to describe their every movement. It was like a real-life whodunnit!

The Austrian police were so friendly and supportive that I felt perfectly safe and had no reason to be nervous.

The only one to suffer was our downhill coach, Wolfgang Bartel, one-time bronze-winner in Innsbruck in 1964. I gained enormously from his experience in the advice which he gave me. For the last few days leading up to the finals, we stayed, not in the Olympic village, but in a small hotel at the foot of the course. This was thanks to our coaches, who alone, among the countries represented, insisted that we be granted this privilege. Wolfgang arrived back rather late; and finding the hotel heavily guarded by dogs, he would not venture inside, but preferred to sleep in his car. But fortunately he did not have long to wait until the morning.

The next murder threat occurred after the Olympics, at the World Cup event in America. I was given four bodyguards — the genuine articles: two coloured, two white, and all four giants. They drove me around in an armoured car. While the other competitors trundled in on the bus, we would shoot past them with our sirens blaring. It was great fun!

Christian naturally came with us, and during the trips he would ask the friendly guards for a full explanation of all their security procedures. He was particularly interested in their radar traps!

The biggest problem occurred during training and in the competition itself, because none of the bodyguards could ski properly. But they were always nearby, slithering about the slope in their shining black boots. They found it highly amusing to have to spend more time on their backsides than on their feet.

One day I invited one of my bodyguards to stand on the tails of my skis so that I could take him down to the bottom of the slope. But he was far too heavy, and we fell spectacularly in the wet spring snow. After we had sorted ourselves out again, the poor chap pulled out his Colt revolver to see if it was still working properly. It produced a cascade of water, just like a tap or a water pistol. The other three were doubled up with laughter.

In Quebec I was forced for security reasons to have a whole floor to myself on the 15th floor of our hotel. I was understandably very lonely up there, but Christian found the ideal solution: he moved into my room to "act as bodyguard" on the basis of the security information he had gleaned in the meantime. But nothing happened . . .

Kitzbühel — the build-up to a competition

(as told by Christian)

Overall winner in the World Cup and twice Olympic gold medallist — those were Rosi's greatest skiing triumphs. But what of mine? Well, I have twice come second and once come third overall in the World Cup slalom; and I have won a World Cup slalom event on six occasions altogether: three times in Wengen, and once in Garmisch, Mégève and Kitzbühel respectively.

I was particularly pleased to win in Kitzbühel, for "Kitz", as it is known, is the most important race of the season. One might even call it the "Monte Carlo" of skiing. It is for this reason that I have chosen the Hahnenkamm race as a typical example of a major skiing event. Here is a description of the week leading up to the race.

The weekend before Kitzbühel

My favourite event, the Lauberhorn race, has been transferred to Crans Montana because of lack of snow; so there are two events in a row at Montana. My luck in Wengen continues to manifest itself in Montana: I win the first race and come fourth in the second. These results are marvellous for my self-confidence, especially in view of the forthcoming event at Kitzbühel, in which I have previously been eliminated as many as eight times in a row.

Monday and Tuesday

I return home to Garmisch-Partenkirchen. In spite of my recent success in Montana, I must now concentrate entirely on the forthcoming event in Kitzbühel, on the basis that the next race is always the most difficult. I never look back, but always look forward to the next challenge. After eight hours' driving it is time for some fitness training, so I slip into tracksuit and do 20 minutes' jogging followed by flexibility exercises.

Tuesday is a day of complete rest and refreshment. In earlier years I would have spent such a day signing autographs or the like, but I stopped this in 1979. Since then it has been a day for switching off completely and recharging the batteries.

Wednesday

Wednesday is the first day of serious training for Sunday. All our resources are concentrated on building up to peak form on that day. We look out a training slope similar to the one at Kitzbühel, and the Olympic slope in Garmisch is suitably steep for the purpose.

We have a small advantage in that our coach Peter Endrass has been involved in the layout of the course at Kitzbühel. This means that we can arrange the poles in the same way for the training runs. We do six runs on this occasion. During the build-up period in the autumn there can often be as many as ten. If this sounds very few, it is worth remembering that

Christian at the slalom in Cortina d'Ampezzo in 1980

149

these runs are extremely demanding, being equivalent to a 400-metre flat run with a pulse rate of up to 220. The runs are interspersed with rests, each being sufficient to make a complete recovery. During these rests we are given massage while we watch our previous run on the video. We can then analyse our faults while they are still fresh in our mind and correct them on the next run.

Lunch is followed by a compulsory rest period, and at four o'clock we go to the gymnasium for condition training, which has also been planned towards Kitzbühel. Today it is strength training. It is still four days before Kitzbühel, so we can afford to build up our reserves of strength as much as possible. This will tire the muscles somewhat, but the effect will have worn off by Sunday. We warm up with a game of football. Football to loosen up, followed by gymnastics: both are compulsory at every training session.

This is followed by further massage in the evening, again with video analysis. And we have the pleasure of going to bed early.

Thursday

Like yesterday, the team gets up at six to get their bodies into the right rhythm for the competition. Breakfast is a large one, but before that comes what in retrospect seems like the most unpleasant part of the whole of a sportsman's career: the daily morning run followed by gymnastics. In winter the temperatures can often be as low as −20 or −25 degrees — but the body must be prepared for the ordeal to come.

By half past nine we are out on the slope, practising all the difficult parts of the "Kitz" course. We finish off with a few "shoots" for good measure. These are short runs, flagged mostly along the fall line, in which all cares are thrown to the wind!

At four o'clock we are back to conditioning, but this time not strength training but a long gymnastics session. We again warm up with a game of football. Thank goodness the downhillers are not present! Then it would be downhill versus slalom, which is quite a tall order!

On Thursday evening I have another look at a video of last year's Hahnenkamm race, to get me mentally prepared for the coming event.

Friday

On Friday we have a sort of dress rehearsal, by practising under race conditions. This consists of four rather shorter runs, each of which is prepared with exactly the same degree of application as the competition itself. We are encouraged to compete full out against one another.

By three o'clock we are already in the gym. Today we are going to concentrate on speed training. We do a number of sprints of different lengths, all of them short but as fast as possible. This is to improve our speed and agility, which is so important for the slalom.

Then follows the journey to Kitzbühel. I can feel the excitement building up as we approach the town and see the course for the first time. There is something quite unforgettable about the atmosphere at Kitzbühel. As a child I used to dream about racing at Kitzbühel. This dream has come true as many as eight times, but never once have I completed the course. And this has been a real nightmare for me.

But as soon as I arrive, Kitzbühel begins to work its magic on me — the fans, the officials, the ski manufacturers, the holiday-makers, the rich men with their beautiful wives, the fast women in their expensive furs, and of course the press. Here they all

are again! For two days there is nothing but racing. The whole world is looking on with the same excitement and anticipation: Japan, Russia, America . . . And yet not all of the people who swarm to Kitzbühel have come for the sport. There are the "jet-setters" who have come to be "seen" here. But how fantastic it feels to be part of it all! The hotel is full of downhillers: their big day is tomorrow. Skiers and coaches are hard at it, discussing the key points of the race and analysing their training performances. The officials, whom I haven't seen since last year, have already predicted the winner, while the press seems more interested in the fact that Franz Klammer takes sweetener instead of sugar in his tea!

In the meantime we slalom skiers have had a short run to loosen our muscles after the journey. We eat our evening meal and go to bed. Our big day is not until the day after tomorrow.

As I drift off to sleep I can think of nothing but the race. My excitement is growing by the hour.

Saturday

Today is the great day for the downhill. We slalom racers are training not far away from the downhill finish, which is already surrounded by thousands of spectators. We do four short runs followed by one "free run". But nobody takes any notice of us. Just before the start of the downhill I go across to a boarding house about 50 yards away belonging to our former coach Ernst Hinterseer, where I watch the race on the television. Hurrah! Sepp Ferstl is the winner!

Back in the hotel, I meet the jubilant German team, together with the even more jubilant Sepp. It's exciting! I think to myself, if only I can do it too!

Now we get back into tracksuits for another fitness session. This time it's specific strength training for the leg, stomach, arm and shoulder muscles. The exercises are strenuous but very short, with only three repetitions at the most. Now the muscles are excited too.

Tonight I can't get to sleep. The Swiss fans with their cowbells are making a dreadful din outside my window. I move into a room on the other side of the hotel. As I go to sleep, I follow the race through in my mind, going slowly at the points where I've previously come to grief.

Sunday — the day of the race

Up at six o'clock sharp for my morning jog. I always take the same route. I wouldn't dare try another on this day of all days. It's one of my many superstitions.

Breakfast doesn't taste as nice as usual; but I'm not really worried: it's better not to overburden the stomach.

I pass the bookmakers' stand on my way to the warm-up session. Stenmark is tipped as the winner, but I'm expected to come second.

After the first few swings I know I'm going to win — it's a foregone conclusion. All around me there are banners and cowbells and photographers. Now it's up to me!

Another hour to wait befor the start! An hour in which to view the course — an hour of concentration, of excitement and of uncertainty. Little do I know how much I shall treasure this moment in later years. I've got the whole course taped: every gate, every jump is engraved in my mind, and I know exactly what my tactics are going to be. Down at the finish, the announcer, one of the best in the business, feeds the excitement of the spectators by calling us to the start.

The first competitor is off. In the meantime I've put on my racing skis, and I try out a few swings to check that the edges are not too sharp. Everything is hectic: the skiers are

given massage while the equipment people check their bindings; the TV journalists try to squeeze the last ounce out of the situation; the coaches talk over the speaker system. Peter my coach gives me a questioning look. He is probably suffering more than I am. I know that paralysing feeling, which has sometimes lost me the race; but the ability to conquer nerves is as much a part of the game as a perfect techique. Only four more to go until number 7, which is my turn. The radio keeps me fully informed. Now at last it is time, and off I go. My nerves evaporate before the first gate, but there remains the determination to show this course what I'm made of. Throughout the run I talk to myself to egg myself on; I hear that I'm making the best time — things are going well; I finish with the best time! The equipment people whisk my skis away, and my colleagues clap me on the shoulders as if I'd already won — but there's another run to go. I escape from them and sit down next to Ernst Hinterseer, where I'm greeted by the sight of a bowl of hot broth.

I have difficulty viewing the second run, with all the loud accompaniment of shouts and cheers: "Christian, you can do it! Bravo! You'll win it this time! Just one autograph, please . . ." But nothing can touch me this time — not even the best times of those racing before me. Today I'm in top form: I defend my lead from the first run, beating Ingemar Stenmark and Phil Mahre to the finish I have always dreamt of.

Superstitions

(as told by Rosi)

Comparing the incident when I broke my skis in Innsbruck with the time when Christian damaged his skis in Wengen, it is obvious that Christian, throughout his career, has been far more vulnerable to external circumstances or faulty equipment than I have. Like many of his colleagues, he must always wear the same cap, the same underwear, the same jumper and the same trousers. Then he can say to himself, "Now everything's as it should be!" Once he had a terrific row with Heinz Krecek, manager of the DSV pool, because the firm whose jumper he wore had withdrawn from the pool, and Heinz had refused to let him start in his old, much-treasured pullover.

Christian almost worshipped his clothing and equipment. For example, if he raced badly twice running with the same cap on, then the third time he had to wear a different one. I seemed to spend my whole life knitting him new caps!

Christian realises only too well these days how bad it is for a sportsman to be so dependent on such things. For the last two years of his racing career, he made conscious efforts to rid himself of this dependence. It is really a question of self-confidence. When you're on the crest of a wave such props are not really important: it is experience and routine which counts. But failure can produce a strong temptation to resort to superstition. And to be perfectly honest, I too used to be extremely superstitious.

There was my golden chain, for example, with my lucky pig on it — a present from Christian. Without it I simply couldn't compete — not under any circumstances! In the World Cup slalom in Cortina, I noticed at the warm-up session that I had left my talisman in my room. I panicked completely and ran all over the place: "Somebody get me a walkie-talkie! Evi's still back in the hotel: I simply *must* radio her to bring it with her!"

But my sister didn't make it in time, and I had to start without my lucky charm. I felt naked. But I still managed to win, so from then on I wore the chain as nothing more than an ornament.

Then there came a time when our coach Heinz Mohr began to preach against the use of such things: they were no more than a distraction and would come to nothing in the end. I took his word for it, but I still kept to one little fad which lay beyond his jurisdiction: my dark-blue tights, without which I never competed . . .

They had already been darned all over, and my mother kept telling me they were no longer decent to wear. What would people think if I had an accident and arrived at the hospital or at the doctor's wearing that bit of old rag? Besides, modern tights were so much better these days. But I remained faithful to these tights, even at the Winter Olympics in Innsbruck.

It is a long jump from Innsbruck to Canada — to Blue River, British Columbia, to be exact. This was to be the location of the so-called "Powder 8 World Championship" of spring 1983, which had been instituted by the helicopter firm "Mike Wiegele". In this championship, two competitors must plunge simultaneously into a beautiful powder slope, and must then produce 120 matching swings to form an exact figure-of-eight pattern in the snow. Christian and I were a pair of raw newcomers, facing hard American competition.

Now this competition is planned entirely as a fun event; but when all is said and done, competition is competition! It pays not to take it too lightly. No wonder, therefore, that Christian was feeling rather nervous at the start. "Don't worry", I whispered to him. "Nothing can go wrong, because I've got my dark-blue tights on today!" The result was that we won!

Rosi and Christian on their World Championship run in Canada in 1983

Photo credits

Bogner, Willy
14, 23

Brownell, David
20, 24b, 82, 86, 87, 111, 121, 132, 134, 144, 153

Buchheim, Yves
109

Bunte Bildarchiv (*Bunte* Picture Archive)
12t, 24t, 129

dpa (German Press Agency)
13b

Harvey, Don
22

Herrgott
88

Hiebeler, Toni
16/17, 21t

Hoppbichler
133, 135

Major, James
31b, 32, 33 (3), 34, 36 (6) 37bl, 40 (2), 43, 44, 45 (2), 46 (3), 47, 48 (6), 49, 50 (4), 51, 52 (2), 53, 54t, 55 (3), 59, 60 (2), 61 (2), 62 (6), 63 (6), 66, 68 (4), 69 (4), 70 (2), 71 (4), 72 (5), 74 (2), 76 (4), 115, 116, 118 (9), 123 (6)

Müller Horst
10b

Neureuther, Christian
10 (2), 56, 89, 140, 143

Perret, Christian
Front and Back Covers and Endpapers
2, 3, 4, 5, 8, 21b, 26, 27, 28, 29, 30, 31t, 37 (2), 39, 41, 42, 54b, 57, 64 (4), 65 (3), 67 (3), 73 (3), 77 (3), 79, 80, 84, 85 (2), 93 (4), 94 (2), 100, 102, 103 (4), 106 (2), 107 (4), 108 (6), 110 (8), 130

Seer, Ulli
81, 83b

Shiga, Zin
18/19, 112, 119, 124/125, 139, 141, 144, 148

Simon, Sven
12, 127b (2)

Ski Magazin:
Bogner, Willy
23
Fausel, J.
13t, 99

Stern: Schmitz, W.
90, 97

Tourist Office, Oetztal
Back endpaper (background)

Werek
11, 38, 78, 127t (2), 142, 151

Index